The Archaeology of North American Farmsteads

The American Experience in Archaeological Perspective

UNIVERSITY PRESS OF FLORIDA

Florida A&M University, Tallahassee
Florida Atlantic University, Boca Raton
Florida Gulf Coast University, Ft. Myers
Florida International University, Miami
Florida State University, Tallahassee
New College of Florida, Sarasota
University of Central Florida, Orlando
University of Florida, Gainesville
University of North Florida, Jacksonville
University of South Florida, Tampa
University of West Florida, Pensacola

The American Experience in Archaeological Perspective
Edited by Michael S. Nassaney

The books in this series explore an event, process, setting, or institution that was significant in the formative experience of contemporary America. Each volume will frame the topic beyond an individual site and attempt to give the reader a flavor of the theoretical, methodological, and substantive issues that researchers face in their examination of that topic or theme. These books will be comprehensive overviews that will allow serious students and scholars to get a good sense of contemporary and past inquiries on a broad theme in American history and culture.

The Archaeology of North American Farmsteads

Mark D. Groover

Foreword by Michael S. Nassaney

University Press of Florida
Gainesville/Tallahassee/Tampa/Boca Raton
Pensacola/Orlando/Miami/Jacksonville/Ft. Myers/Sarasota

Copyright 2008 by Mark D. Groover
Printed in the United States of America on recycled, acid-free paper
All rights reserved

13 12 11 10 09 08 6 5 4 3 2 1

Library of Congress Cataloging-in-Publication Data
ISBN 978-0-8130-3263-4

The University Press of Florida is the scholarly publishing agency for the State
University System of Florida, comprising Florida A&M University, Florida Atlantic
University, Florida Gulf Coast University, Florida International University, Florida
State University, New College of Florida, University of Central Florida, University of
Florida, University of North Florida, University of South Florida, and University of
West Florida.

University Press of Florida
15 Northwest 15th Street
Gainesville, FL 32611-2079
http://www.upf.com

For Anna, Nicholas, and Mary

Contents

Figures

Tables

Foreword

Growing up just outside Providence, Rhode Island, in an urban setting, my first experience with an agrarian landscape came in 1978 when I worked on the FAI-270 archaeological mitigation project in the American Bottom of Illinois. As soon as I joined my field supervisor and crew at a threatened site overlooking the bottomlands, I was given a handful of pin flags and told to mark the locations of surface artifacts. I had never conducted a pedestrian survey and defensively retorted, "where I come from we *dig* for our archaeology!" My new associates quickly concluded that my hire was a mistake. Although I had heard that plowed fields were good places to find Indian artifacts, as a boy I neither hunted for arrowheads nor even walked in an agricultural field. Of course, most of New England was once farmland, and a year later I was recording many old plowzone profiles in another highway mitigation project (I-495 in southeast Massachusetts), lamenting the damage that agricultural activities had done to the archaeological record. Farm abandonment in New England began in the late eighteenth century, and developments associated with nineteenth-century industry nearly completed the process. Subsequent industrial growth and urban sprawl destroyed evidence of these colonial and antebellum sites well before federal legislation required that they be identified and evaluated to determine their historical significance.

The processes that contributed to the decline of the family farm and the growth of agribusiness accelerated and peaked in the early twentieth century, resulting in a dramatic transformation across the American landscape with profound implications for the economic, social, and material conditions of life. At the Warren B. Shepard farmstead site that I investigated in Battle Creek, Michigan, farming was terminated in 1904 when Shephard's daughters subdivided and began selling parcels of what had been a prosperous 120-acre farm for nearly 75 years. Indeed, most Americans know that farming is a vanishing way of life. The result for historical archaeologists is the hundreds if not thousands of abandoned farmsteads that comprise an archaeological legacy representative of the way we were. While farmsteads are often seen as a mundane and redundant site type, the case can be made that their archaeological study can contribute to a better understanding of the agrarian foundations of the American experience.

In *The Archaeology of North American Farmsteads*, Mark Groover explores the archaeological potential for this unique site type and advocates the need to consolidate and synthesize information on the material remains of a bygone way of life to gain insight into this passing chapter of American history and culture. As Groover notes, American farms were once ubiquitous and numbered over 2 million immediately after the Civil War. It was the opening of the frontier in the late eighteenth and early nineteenth centuries that facilitated agricultural expansion. Yet, the future of agrarian America was in question as early as the beginning of the nineteenth century, when industrialization took hold and grew. By the middle of the nineteenth century, expansion was made commercially feasible by improved transportation networks that brought western and midwestern products to cities and eastern markets. While large segments of the population lived or worked on farms well into the nineteenth century, technological innovations such as mechanization began replacing human labor at an increasing rate in the early twentieth century, resulting in fewer but larger commercial farms. These trends have accelerated over the past 50 years by consolidation and other forces that made agribusiness profitable.

Because farmsteads were linked to the market and often were occupied for long periods of time, they are sensitive barometers to assess changes in broader cultural processes of industrialization, immigration, and consumerism. As Groover demonstrates, these global processes varied in the degree to which they were embraced or resisted over time, through space, and by particular households. To illustrate the utility of the American farm as an analytical unit, Groover examines a series of case studies including a variety of farmstead types in the eastern United States from the seventeenth century through the 1950s. He presents a useful research framework for investigating these sites and determining how to evaluate their historical significance. His survey shows that farmsteads have not been ignored, though an overarching framework to organize their study has been lacking. The approach he advocates will be a welcome addition to the literature because farmsteads are often encountered in cultural resource management studies yet their archaeological potential has often been overlooked. While Groover's cases are drawn from the East, they are broadly applicable for understanding farming wherever it was adopted and relinquished.

The passing of historic preservation laws in the 1960s and 1970s has mandated the investigation of sites associated with all Americans, regardless of social class, gender, race, ethnicity, or location—sites in both urban and rural settings are of potential interest. Despite these efforts to be inclusive, the idea that farming represented an idyllic and isolated way of life (the "Agrarian Myth") has been difficult to dispel and has fostered an image of stasis and homogeneity. Yet, studies have shown that farm households during the early modern period were enmeshed in intricate commercial systems with links to broader popular culture trends and consumer products well beyond their front porches.

The plethora of archaeological remains of farmstead sites has never been in doubt. What emerges from Groover's study is the idea that farmsteads are as abundant as they are variable in form and content. Dimensions of material variability that inform on past lifeways include architectural forms (house size and method of construction); spatial organization (locations of outbuildings and disposal areas); subsistence remains (animal species composition and butchering practices); and objects of consumer culture associated with food preparation, health, and status display (ceramics and patent medicine bottles), among others. Divergent patterns of adoption suggest that the American experience on the farm was by no means homogeneous, and much can be learned from examining the articulation between large-scale processes of modernization and their local material expressions.

Agriculture was repeatedly adopted in many parts of the world long before Europeans began practicing it in America, and it has had a profound influence on human history. A small but significant part of that history involves the investigation of America's deep agricultural roots. Historical archaeologists are well poised to study the development, expansion, and decline of our nation's agricultural heritage. By examining farmsteads within the context of long-term history, archaeologists can contribute to a better understanding of the threads that connect the past with the present and provide a clearer sense of the struggles, successes, and failures represented by the material remains of farms on the American landscape. Such a perspective brings into focus the countless and changing ways in which America was created, lived, and experienced.

Michael S. Nassaney
Series Editor

Preface and Acknowledgments

I have been fortunate to study the historical archaeology of rural life. Along the way this research interest has been encouraged and influenced by a number of people. In 1987, during my junior year as an undergraduate anthropology student at the University of Tennessee in Knoxville, I participated in excavations at the Gibbs house. Fieldwork at the Gibbs site, directed by Charles Faulkner, was my first foray into farmstead archaeology. A few years later, I conducted excavations at the Thomas Howell plantation near Columbia, a colonial rural site, under the direction of Leland Ferguson with the University of South Carolina. Forming a crew of two, colleague Melanie Cabak helped me with the excavations at the Howell site. Later, Melanie and I worked with Charles Orser and David Babson at Illinois State University. Melanie and I conducted excavations at several midwest farmsteads and at Wessyngton, a tobacco plantation near Nashville. During conversations with Chuck and David, we learned about the dilemma of farms in historical archaeology, especially in regions where archaeologically encountered farmsteads were often not older than a century (or less). A few years later, I returned to the University of Tennessee and continued my work on the Gibbs farmstead under the guidance of Charles Faulkner. I collaborated on the *Old Farm, New Farm* report with Melanie at the Savannah River Archaeological Research Program (SRARP). I also later collaborated on *Living on the Edge* and *Plantations without Pillars* at the SRARP. Considered together, these individuals and research experiences have contributed significantly to my on-going interest in the historical archaeology of rural life.

In 2004, Michael Nassaney asked me to contribute to The American Experience in Archaeological Perspective book series. I sincerely thank Michael for this opportunity, and I appreciate his guidance and patience during this project. I also thank George "Buddy" Wingard at the Savannah River Archaeological Research Program, University of South Carolina, for drafting the figures in the book. Figure 1.2 was drafted by Angela Gibson in the Geospatial Center and Map Collection at Ball State University. Financial support for the graphics in the book was provided by a grant from the Ball State University Office of the Provost for Academic Research. I thank Mary Carter and Lynne Cooper at Ball State University for their grant support.

I also thank Donald Hardesty and Barbara Little for reviewing the book manuscript and providing constructive comments and suggestions. Editors Eli Bortz and Heather Romans with the University Press of Florida were also very helpful, and I thank them for their guidance with the manuscript preparation. Colleen Boyd, John Boyd, Jim Connolly, Eric Lassiter, Rob Quinlan, and Marsha Quinlan provided support as colleagues during the completion of this writing project. Last, I thank Melanie for her encouragement and suggestions over the years.

Why Study Farm Sites?

Farming: An Ancient Legacy

From humble beginnings, human life on planet Earth has been characterized by a succession of major events. In the jungles and across the grasslands of East Africa, our ancient hominid ancestors had begun walking on two legs by 5 million years ago. By 2 million years ago, the first crude stone tools had been invented. A short time later (ca. 1.7 million years ago), the first migrations out of Africa occurred. Approximately 190,000 years ago, modern humans living in hunting and gathering societies (human groups that depend upon wild animals and plants for survival) evolved in East Africa, and by 40,000 years ago modern groups began colonizing all inhabitable parts of the planet. Between 30,000 to 15,000 years ago, the distinctive material culture of modern humans became increasingly prevalent in the archaeological record, characterized by the use of sophisticated utilitarian items, such as the spear thrower and finely made stone tools. During this time our expressive culture also took flight, with the appearance of the first art on the walls of caves and rock shelters, the widespread use of items for personal adornment, participation in long-distance trade systems, and increasingly complex burial practices.

With the end of the Ice Age 10,000 years ago, ancient humans came up with a new invention—farming. This seemingly simple practice was a major transition in human development, and it continues to have a profound influence on the world we inhabit today. Farming was an independent invention that appeared in many different places over time after 10,000 years ago. Today archaeologists understand that agriculture started through a complex cultural and biological process called artificial selection—an early form of biological engineering—in which ancient farmers selected desirable characteristics in plants and animals that they raised. This mutually beneficial process over time created domesticates—animals and plants that through human intervention have become genetically altered from their wild predecessors. Today, biologists and archaeologists understand the process of domestication, but the reasons people started farming in the first place are less clear and represent an issue of vigorous debate in archaeology. Most contemporary archaeologists agree that agriculture came about through a complex interplay of different factors: The right environmental conditions, increasing human population and decreasing wild food resources, the tendency of humans to live in smaller and smaller territories over time, and increasing social complexity all contributed to the development of agriculture.

Although the exact mechanisms responsible for farming are still being explored and clarified by archaeologists, one fact is clear: Many of the early farming societies that appeared shortly after the Ice Age quickly matured into some of the first agricultural civilizations. Called agricultural states by archaeologists, complex farming cultures after 5,000 years ago developed on practically all continents: in Mesopotamia (modern-day Iraq and Iran), in North Africa in Egypt, in India, China, and, a little later, in Central and South America. Much of modern life draws upon cultural and technological advances first invented by these ancient agricultural civilizations—writing, math, calendars, astronomy, engineering, and a broad range of expressive cultural practices such as elaborate art, literature, theater, music, and a plethora of craft traditions: metal working, lapidary, and textile manufacture, to name a few (Feder 2007).

Ancient agricultural societies have waxed and waned throughout the world, with many existing in relative isolation, until another major event occurred in human history—the European discovery of the New World that marked the beginning of the modern era approximately 500 years ago. After European seafarers happened upon the Americas in the late 1400s, the world started to become a much smaller place, and a fascinating process of cultural cross-fertilization commenced that today continues unabated. People from the Old World, particularly Europeans, began inhabiting the Americas. Through forced migration, enslaved people from West and Central Africa were also brought to the New World. These Old World travelers in turn encountered diverse Native American cultures. Within this dynamic crucible of cultural interaction, from small farms operated by settler families to large plantations worked by hundreds of enslaved laborers, agriculture encouraged settlement and sustained the developing economy in the New World. Until recently, farming has remained a predominant way of life in the United States.

Farming in America: A Vanishing Way of Life

In the United States, farming households settled the Atlantic coast in the early 1600s and reached the Pacific West by the late 1800s. This period witnessed the development of farms from subsistence-oriented operations using mainly human and animal labor, intended to sustain individual farming households, to the growth of large-scale commercial farms operated by capital-intensive agricultural machinery. The twentieth century in turn was characterized by the gradual decline of the family-operated farm, especially after the close of World War II.

Beginning in 1850, the U.S. government began recording the number of farms in the census. Figure 1.1 clearly illustrates the quantitative history of the American farm. In 1850 there were 1.4 million farms in America. Seventy years later in 1920 the number of farms in the country peaked at 6.4 million and immediately began to decline. At the end of the twentieth century, farm decline leveled off to 2.1 million in 1990 and 2000. In 2000 the number

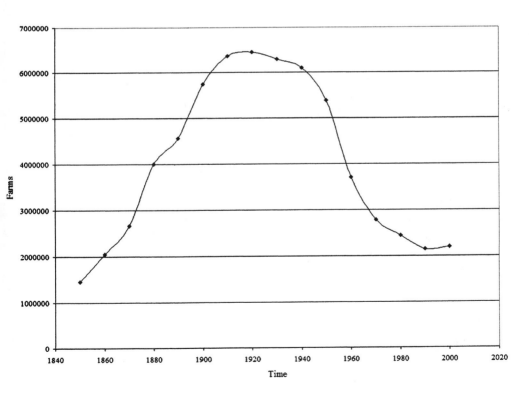

Figure 1.1. Number of U.S. farms, 1850–2000.

of farms was approximately the same as the number of farms in 1860 on the eve of the Civil War (United States Bureau of the Census [USBC] 1853; United States Department of Agriculture [USDA] 1997, 2002; United States Department of Commerce [USDC] 1913, 1922, 1932, 1942, 1952, 1959, 1964, 1982; United States Department of Interior [USDI] 1864, 1872, 1883, 1895, 1902).

As illustrated by census records, an important chapter of American history is drawing to a close. Farms will never disappear in America, but the gradual decline of family-operated farms in the United States during the past 150 years is a historical fact (Fite 1981; Friedberger 1988). Consequently, within the past half-century Americans have experienced the end of an agricultural era. Today, many parents and grandparents grew up on farms in American families, yet younger generations only know of this historically significant way of life through family stories. As the prevalence of the family-operated farm diminishes in contemporary America, it becomes increasingly important to study and document this important part of the American experience. Historical archaeology, the study of the recent past using artifacts and historical records, is well suited to helping better understand and document the history, culture, and material culture of American farms during the past 400 years.

Historical archaeologists have studied farms since the 1960s and 1970s. Archaeological excavations at farms reveal important cultural information about people who lived during the recent past. The insights gained from farmstead archaeology—the layout of house lots and dwellings that farm families resided in, the types of outbuildings they constructed, the crops they raised, the types of food they ate, and the range of store-bought goods that they used on a daily basis—are often not readily available from other information sources. Besides important information related to specific farm families, the archaeology of farmsteads provides significant anthropological knowledge about cultural trends and processes that occurred in the United States.

For example, by looking at the entire history of the eastern United States, historical archaeologists are confronted with several important, recurring trends that influenced the character of rural life and the development of the nation. Colonization and frontier settlement are significant processes that historical archaeologists often address at specific sites. How were pioneer life and frontier farming similar or different in regions across the nation? Did immigrant pioneers reestablish familiar cultural practices in America, such as farm layout, dwelling styles, and foodways, or can we see changes in the material conditions of settler households? As frontier conditions diminished in different regions, rural households also often began to produce farm surpluses and engage in commercial agriculture. Archaeologically, what does this transition to commercial farming look like at different sites? Can we detect improvements in architecture and the standard of living among farm families as their agricultural operations became commercially oriented? Conversely, not all farm households were successful. What does farm failure look like archaeologically? By the middle of the 1800s, mechanization and progressive farming practices also began to influence rural life. These changes have a strong material component and can potentially be identified archaeologically. Finally, what does the decline of a predominant way of life like farming look like across the landscape? Landscape approaches and settlement studies in historical archaeology are well suited to reconstruct the process of out-migration and farmstead consolidation that occurred in rural areas during the late 1800s and into the first half of the twentieth century.

In addition to these large-scale processes that transpired across America, farmstead studies also reveal relevant cultural information about the details of daily rural life. Called cultural continuity, some settler households transplanted Old World material traditions and strove to maintain culturally distinct practices in the New World. Conversely, over time other farming families and rural communities embraced culture change and voluntarily adjusted to new circumstances in America. Further, Native American households and African American households experienced a broad range of social and material challenges in rural contexts that other cultural groups did not experience, such as forced relocation, violence, and discriminatory racial practices. These experiences in turn significantly influenced the character of daily life at rural sites inhabited by Native Americans and African Americans. Consequently, the range of living conditions, social change (or continuity), and social challenges that rural households experienced are aptly revealed through archaeology and the study of material culture.

Farm Sites: A Prevalent Archaeological Resource

Most historians and social scientists recognize that farming is an important part of American history and culture. Coinciding with the creation of national preservation laws, especially the National Historic Preservation Act, since the late 1970s archaeologists have continued to grapple with the issue of how to effectively manage and interpret farm sites (Adams 1980; Stewart-Abernathy 1986; Stine 1989; Orser 1990; Wilson 1990; Cabak and Inkrot 1997; Groover 1998, 2003; Cabak et al. 1999; Hardesty and Little 2000; Hart and Fisher 2000; Baugher and Klein 2003; Sayers 2003; De Cunzo 2004). Farm sites present archaeologists with unique field and management challenges for two interrelated reasons: abundance and age. Perhaps most important, in many areas of the United States farmstead sites are abundant archaeological resources. Based on the previously discussed census of agriculture information, millions of farmsteads were established and eventually abandoned between 1850 and 1950, not to mention those established, occupied, and abandoned from the seventeenth through the mid-nineteenth centuries. Consequently, during routine archaeological surveys an appreciable number of farm sites are often discovered, to the extent that archaeologists conducting and administrating cultural resource management studies sometimes view farmsteads as representing a redundant and expendable archaeological resource possessing minimal information potential (Hardesty and Little 2000: 119–131, 156–159).

In addition to abundance, many farmstead sites, from an archaeological perspective, are not very old. In many regions, farm sites dating to the colonial or early federal periods (from the 1600s to the early 1800s) are rare and not routinely discovered during archaeological surveys. However, more recent farm sites, especially those less than 150 years old, dramatically increase in abundance in many parts of the United States. As illustrated in agricultural census information, this prominent increase in the prevalence of late nineteenth and twentieth-century farms is due principally to the process of geographic infilling over time, in which rural populations grew in size as younger households in second and third generation farm families sought to create their own farms. Unfortunately, many of these sites are often dismissed as archaeologically insignificant.

Despite the challenges presented by the issues of farmstead abundance and age, in this book I emphasize that the archaeology of farmsteads is an important and relevant topic in the related areas of historical archaeology, cultural resource management studies, anthropology in general, and American social history. The potential information that these archaeological resources offer is limited only by the research designs and research questions posed by archaeologists. Further, since archaeology is a science of time and material culture, careful scrutiny of the archaeological record encountered at historic farm sites may reveal unanticipated information pertaining to cultural processes, landscape change, and rural household dynamics. This information may be relevant not only to historical archaeologists but also to colleagues in history, cultural anthropology, cultural geography, and folk life studies, to name a few.

With these thoughts in mind, the purpose of this book is to explore archaeologically the material legacy of farming in the United States. *The Archaeology of North American Farmsteads* is not meant to be a definitive, final statement about the topic, but rather a contribution to the continuing dialogue on the topic that has been ongoing since the 1980s. Consequently, this book aims to provide an introduction to the topic for historical archaeology students and offer potentially useful ideas to archaeologists who routinely encounter farmsteads while conducting fieldwork.

The format of this book uses a culture history and culture region approach (Table 1.1). The purpose of this format is to illustrate prevalent material trends in the archaeology of farms during different time periods and in different regions. The temporal and geographic focus of this book is the archaeology of farmsteads occupied between the 1600s and 1950s in the eastern United States. The history of farms in America is divided into the colonial (ca. 1600s to late 1700s), antebellum (ca. 1800–1865), and postbellum/modern periods (ca. 1865–1950). Archaeological examples of farms inhabited in the Northeast, Southeast, and Midwest in the eastern United States during these culture history periods are discussed in the book.

Prevalent research themes in farmstead studies are summarized in chapter 2, and a research design for farmstead archaeology is presented. Using ideas related to time scales from the *Annales* School of French social historians and concepts developed in world systems theory, it is proposed that archaeologists should attempt to systematically define the main economic and material characteristics of farms in different regions through time using fine-grained contextual frameworks. The larger purpose of this effort is to identify through syntheses the major regional material trends in the history and archaeology of American farms. Seemingly an unrealistically ambitious project, a large amount of extant archaeological data related to farmsteads already exists in many parts of the United States. Related to regionally based research designs and syntheses, issues pertaining to research significance and the archaeological evaluation of farmstead sites are also discussed in chapter 2. It is suggested that by eventually synthesizing the previous 25 to 30 years of farmstead archaeology, historical archaeologists can more effectively manage, preserve, and study this type of archaeological resource in the future.

Containing case studies that illustrate research trends and themes in the archaeology of farmsteads, chapters 3 through 5 are divided chronologi-

Table 1.1. Farming Regions, Time Periods, and Sites Discussed in Text

Time Period	Region	Site/Area
Colonial	Northeast	William Strickland farm
Colonial	Southeast	Kingsmill
Colonial	Midwest	French Illinois Country
Federal/Antebellum	Northeast	Shaeffer farm
Federal/Antebellum	Southeast	Gibbs farm
Federal/Antebellum	Midwest	Shepard farm
Postbellum/20th century	Northeast	Porter farm
Postbellum/20th century	Southeast	Savannah River valley
Postbellum/20th century	Midwest	Drake farm

cally by culture periods and regions (Figure 1.2). The sites featured in these chapters are intended to illustrate interesting archaeological examples of farmstead studies and the different types of farms that existed in the eastern United States between the 1600s and 1950s. The examples demonstrate that a broad range of different farm types existed in the United States during the recent past, underscoring the complexity of the topic. Farms were operated by families of different ethnicities, races, nationalities, and religious orientations. Household characteristics likewise could profoundly influence the material record at farms. At a basic level, farmsteads were operated by families who practiced a production-consumption economy. They produced most of the foodstuffs that they consumed and depended upon household, family-based labor to raise farm products. Likewise, farm sites usually contain a square or rectangular house lot, architectural features such as dwelling and outbuilding remains, fence lines, and refuse disposal areas.

In addition to material characteristics, the distinction between farms and plantations in the South during the colonial period can be problematic and confusing. In this book, plantations are considered to be composed of large landholdings, encompassing hundreds of acres that were worked by large numbers of enslaved laborers, usually on the order of 50 to 100 or more individuals. Formal, large-scale plantations are not addressed in this study. Conversely, as discussed in chapter 3, many agricultural operations existed in the Tidewater region of colonial Virginia and other parts of the South that contained a European settler household and a small number of enslaved Africans. European settlers during the colonial period often called these rural residences "plantations," when in reality they were small farms that were worked by a small number of slaves. An important part of the

Figure 1.2. Location of sites discussed in text.

colonial South, farms worked by a small number of slaves are consequently addressed in chapter 3.

As illustrated by the examples presented in this book, farm families experienced a wide range of economic situations and material conditions. Adopting a commercial orientation, some farm families owned the land they worked, such as the Shepard farm in the antebellum Midwest, and they sought to get ahead financially and enjoy profits from their agricultural efforts. Other farm families did not own land but labored as tenant farmers, such as tenants and indentured servants on tobacco farms in the colonial Chesapeake or postbellum tenants on cotton farms along the Savannah River valley. Likewise, some farms illustrate rural success stories of upward mobility in which landless farm laborers rose through the agricultural ranks and became wealthy landowners over time, as illustrated by the William Strickland farm in central Delaware during the middle 1700s. Other farms were almost religiously maintained and occupied by the same extended family over several generations for a century or more, as occurred at the Gibbs farm in East Tennessee. And although the men in farm families are often thought to have been the persons in charge of farm operations, the Drake site in Illinois illustrates that farmwives often exercised considerable economic influence in the households they helped sustain. In sum, the archaeological case studies assembled in this book highlight the broad range of cultural, economic, and material conditions that farm families experienced in the eastern United States between the 1600s and 1950s.

As discussed in chapters 2 and 6 regarding the future of farmstead archaeology, the challenge for historical archaeologists is to systematically define the range of material characteristics and conditions that rural families experienced in America during the historic past. This goal will not only provide enhanced insight into the material lives and culture of rural families but will also help to manage more effectively the archaeological record preserved at the countless farmsteads located across the United States.

2

The Archaeology of Farmsteads and Rural Life

Previous Research Topics in Farmstead Archaeology

The sites studied by historical archaeologists range from rural settings to urban locations. Urban archaeologists investigate the development of cities and urban life. Conversely, the historical archaeology of rural contexts encompasses those aspects of American life that have occurred outside of cities and towns. Farmstead archaeology is a research area within the larger topic of the historical archaeology of rural contexts (Adams 1990). Starting from humble beginnings in the late 1960s and early 1970s, some of the first archaeological investigations of rural life focused upon the study of plantations and sites inhabited by enslaved African Americans in the South (e.g., Ascher and Fairbanks 1971; Fairbanks 1972, 1984). This topic has subsequently expanded into one of the most productive and organized research areas in the historical archaeology of rural contexts (Singleton 1988, 1995; Singleton and Bograd 1995). The reason for this information florescence is because this topic is well suited for maximizing the interpretive potential associated with the historical archaeology of inadequately documented contexts (Deagan 1982; Little 1994). Through the study of plantations, historical archaeology has achieved stature as a primary information source associated with the topic of slavery, particularly in the domain of material life and culture.

Living conditions, housing and spatial arrangements, foodways, artifact patterning, and belief systems are frequently addressed topics in plantation archaeology (Singleton 1988, 1995; Singleton and Bograd 1995). Studies focusing upon architecture, diet, household items, and health have provided a detailed composite portrait of slavery. The sum total of previous studies suggests that scholars exploring the topic should avoid simple or broad generalizations. The results generated from the efforts of archaeologists indicate there was not a universal experience among enslaved African Americans in the domain of material life but rather a wide range of individual experiences that were dependent upon numerous variables and situations. Variables that undoubtedly influenced the living conditions of enslaved African Americans include the economic position, ethnicity, and nationality of planters; the plantation production type, size, and associated labor systems; the use of nucleated or dispersed residence patterns; and the location of enslaved individuals within the plantation occupational hierarchy.

In addition to living conditions and the immediate domestic environment, other prominent topics in plantation studies are power relations as expressed through material culture and the built environment (Orser 1988a), the participation of slaves in informal economies (Adams and Boling 1989), the construction of racism and racial identity (Babson 1990), the survival and transformation of West African–influenced cultural elements (Ferguson 1992), cultural interface and exchange between ethnic groups (Groover 1991, 1992a, 1994, 2000), and the transformation of African-influenced belief systems (Ferguson 1992; Stine et al. 1996).

Research topics have expanded in African-American archaeology since the 1990s (e.g., Singleton 1995; Orser 1998; Leone et al. 2005) and consist of studies associated with empowerment, economic and social advancement among African Americans, the development of community institutions during the postbellum and modern periods, and the material construction and negotiation of racial categories (e.g., Cabak et al. 1995; Mullins 1999; Baumann 2001). Recent topics in African-American archaeology have also focused on participation among the public and descendant groups in recovering and interpreting the African-American past (Cabak et al. 1995; McDavid and Babson 1997; Baumann 2001), engendering African-American archaeology (Cabak and Young 1998; Wilkie 2003; Galle and Young 2004), and continuing interest in the archaeological expressions of African-American belief systems (Leone and Fry 1999; Stine et al. 2000; Leone 2005: 192–244).

Ironically, although farmsteads represent one of the most prevalent type of sites in North America (Friedlander 1991), they have yet to foster a fully organized and conscious research effort, like the research impetus associated with plantation and African-American archaeology. The main reason for the lack of a fully developed identity in farmstead archaeology is perhaps because many archaeologists have been hesitant to recognize the topic as a distinct research domain in historical archaeology. In combination with this lack of identity or direction, the absence of an informal network between researchers has likewise perhaps hindered the formalization of the topic. Many historical archaeologists have diligently worked on rural sites in relative isolation in different parts of the country without a substantial level of collaboration or communication with individuals conducting similar field research. In contrast, African-American archaeology, since it focuses upon a Diaspora topic, has been galvanized by the neglected topics of African-American history and culture in North America in combination with the information potential that archaeology can bring to bear on these studies. Farm sites are often considered mundane with limited research potential. Further, twentieth-century sites were not always considered to be "old enough" to be of archaeological interest when preservation legislation was passed in the 1960s and 1970s.

Despite the absence of an organized research identity, during the past twenty years the material life and living conditions of farm families in North America have nonetheless become clearer and more focused owing to the collective efforts of many historical archaeologists. Mainly because of the growth of cultural resource management (CRM) studies, farmsteads have become increasingly encountered during fieldwork and have subsequently become the subject of excavation projects. The increase in CRM studies has likewise created the quandary of how to manage farm sites effectively. Within farmstead archaeology, a diverse range of research questions has been considered. As a means of systematically considering the questions archaeologists have asked at farmsteads, a bibliography compiled by Peggy Beedle (1996: 111–143) offers a relevant starting point for examining the development of research topics and themes in farmstead archaeology. Her bibliography presents a sample of farmstead studies drawn from conference papers, compliance reports, refereed and nonrefereed journal articles, and books. The author divides the bibliography on farmstead archaeology by geographic regions: New England, the Middle Atlantic, the South, the Midwest, the Plains, and Canada. Each section contains reference citations along with abstracts for more recent studies.

To identify prevalent research trends in farmstead archaeology over time, quantitative analysis of the bibliography (Beedle 1996) was conducted with methods similar to those utilized by Smith (1996) in a bibliography on historical archaeology in Tennessee. For analysis of Beedle's bibliography, the number of reports by region and time period was first quantified. The distribution of research themes by category was likewise tabulated. It is assumed that the bibliography is not a complete listing of all farmstead studies in historical archaeology; rather it is primarily intended to serve as a reference source for archaeologists conducting research in Wisconsin. However, Beedle (1996: 7) notes that works related to states and regions that contributed settlers to Wisconsin were also included. Although this source is over a

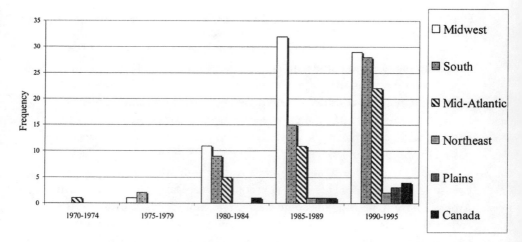

Figure 2.1. Distribution of farmstead studies by geographic regions.

decade old, it nonetheless includes a large number of farmstead studies (ca. 170). Consequently, it is assumed that it contains a valid and representative citation sample for identifying general research trends associated with the topic of farmstead archaeology in the United States.

Concerning the diachronic distribution of farmstead studies by region, the results suggest that in North America's archaeological literature this research topic was represented sporadically in all geographic divisions during the 1970s (Figure 2.1). Paralleling the formalization of historical archaeology as a recognized subdiscipline in anthropology, the first stirrings of farmstead archaeology occurred between 1980 and 1984 with the Midwest and South leading the nation in farmstead studies. Compared to these regions, the Middle Atlantic region trailed by half in the number of historical archaeology studies devoted to farmsteads. Unfortunately, New England, the Plains, and Canada have been consistently underrepresented in farmstead research since the 1980s. This trend could merely be the result of sampling bias on the part of the bibliography compiler; conversely, it could also be real, suggesting, unfortunately, that farm sites in these regions have been compromised without adequate archaeological study.

Between 1985 and 1990, the number of farmstead studies tripled for the Midwest and doubled for the South and the Middle Atlantic states from the previous period of 1980–1984. Also, the regional rank order for the number of studies during this period is the Midwest, the South, and the Middle Atlantic. Again, this distribution may be because of sampling bias based on the location of the compiler and her access to available reports. Conversely, the data could be valid, which would suggest that between 1980 and 1989 most farmstead studies were conducted in the Midwest.

Between 1990 and 1995, two significant events occurred: The number of farmstead studies in the Midwest declined, and the number of farmstead studies conducted between the Midwest, South, and Middle Atlantic states became equal. Between 1990 and 1995, the number of rural studies declined from the 1985–1989 interval for the Midwest yet increased in the South and the Middle Atlantic states. Overall, the number of studies by region became approximately equal between 1990 and 1995.

These temporal and regional trends suggest that the past twenty years have witnessed the birth (ca. 1980–1984), adolescence (ca. 1985–1989), and subsequent maturation or formalization (ca. 1990–present) of farmstead studies, especially in the Midwest, the South, and the Middle Atlantic states. Although a large number of archaeology field reports have been written about farmstead archaeology, the appearance of thematic journal issues (e.g., Orser 1990; Baugher and Klein 2003), a bibliography on the subject (Beedle 1996), several theses and dissertations (Stine 1989; Groover 1998; Sayers 1999), and books (Hardesty and Little 2000: 119–132; Hart and Fisher 2000; Baugher and Klein 2003; Groover 2003; De Cunzo 2004) on the topic likewise indicate that the historical archaeological community has begun to recognize the importance of farmstead archaeology as a distinct research subject.

In addition to temporal trends, the bibliography compiled by Beedle also illustrates prevalent research topics typically addressed in farmstead archaeology. Since a large number of abstracts were not included in the bibliography, analysis of research themes by region or time period was not conducted. Rather, the abstracts were tabulated by general topic. The most prevalent farmstead topics identified from a sample of 51 abstracts by category (Figure 2.2) for the period 1980–1996 include landscape studies (41 percent, n=21), socioeconomic status studies (18 percent, n=9), and regional studies (8 percent, n=4). These three topics represent about two-thirds of the abstract sample.

Landscape studies at rural sites (e.g., Paynter 1982; Adams 1990; Kelso and Most 1990; King 1994; Yamin and Metheny 1996; Rotman and Nassaney 1997; Stine et al. 1997; Nassaney et al. 2001) consist of those archaeological investigations that focus upon defining the land use, domestic architecture,

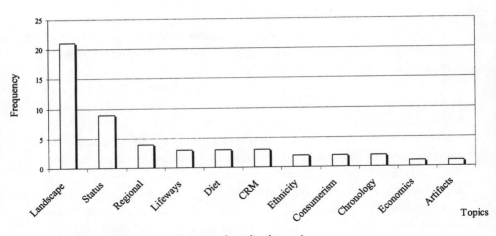

Figure 2.2. Distribution of farmstead studies by topics.

arrangement of outbuildings and fences, feature types, or general site structure associated with a given farmstead. Similar to the concept of site phasing in British archaeology (Clarke 2001), landscape studies usually possess a diachronic dimension, and researchers often attempt to define the sequence of landscape events that transpired at a residence in relation to its known occupational history (e.g., Nassaney et al. 2001; Groover 2004).

Status studies (Orser 1988b) typically address the material wealth held by the residents of a site, variously defined as socioeconomic status, socioeconomic class, or rural tenure class. Socioeconomic status as an analysis variable was used widely during the 1980s, whereas socioeconomic or rural tenure class as analysis variables are more prevalent in the literature since the 1990s (e.g., Cabak and Inkrot 1997; Cabak et al. 1999), especially for farm studies. Research addressing socioeconomic class and status often involves intersite comparison of assemblages between different occupation periods or households and between assemblages from different sites occupied by different social classes.

Upland South studies (e.g., McCorvie 1987; McCorvie et al. 1989; Groover 1993; Smith 1993) were placed in the regional category. These studies, prevalent during the 1980s and early to middle 1990s, relied upon an interpretive model borrowed from cultural geography (Walker and Haag 1974). The model, similar to the culture region concept used by prehistoric cultural historians, mainly consists of a list of attributes or a checklist interpreted to represent a regional folk tradition. The remaining third of the abstract sample consists of secondary research topics. These topics include reconstructing rural lifeways (n=3), defining diet from faunal remains (n=3), assessing site significance (n=3), examining ethnicity (n=2), investigating consumerism (n=2), exploring economic development (n=1) and conducting artifact studies (n=1).

In summary, this brief review indicates that prominent research topics in farmstead archaeology consist of landscape studies (e.g., Paynter 1982; Adams 1990; Kelso and Most 1990; King 1994; Yamin and Metheny 1996; Rotman and Nassaney 1997; Stine et al. 1997; Nassaney et al. 2001) and examining the variables that influenced creation of site structure and the material record. Socioeconomic status, tenure class, race, gender, and ethnicity (Jurney and Moir 1987; Moir and Jurney 1987; Jurney et al. 1988; Stine 1989, 1990; Joseph et al. 1991; Mascia 1994, 1996) are prevalent topics in farmstead studies.

Concerning the relationship between wealth and material conditions, several key studies in rural archaeology indicate that differences in the living conditions experienced by different tenure, racial, or ethnic groups were usually most pronounced or visible in the area of the built environment and domestic dwellings (Horn 1988; Friedlander 1991; Nassaney et al. 2001). In contrast, the archaeologically recovered portable material culture used by different rural wealth or tenure groups often does not conform to simple generalizations. As demonstrated by several studies, lower wealth groups often possessed a similar range of archaeologically represented consumer goods in comparison to middle and upper wealth groups (Orser 1988a; Stine 1989, 1990; Joseph et al. 1991; Cabak and Inkrot 1997; Cabak et al. 1999). However, the use of national or popular, as opposed to folk, architectural styles, the acquisition of new household technology, and the adoption of mechanized farming practices and equipment were typically restricted to affluent, rural households (Cabak and Inkrot 1997; Cabak et al. 1999).

Other important topics in farmstead archaeology not included in Beedle's bibliography consist of settlement studies (Paynter 1982; Brooks 1987; Linebaugh and Robinson 1994), identifying the effects of consumerism and market networks on rural households (Stewart-Abernathy 1986), and defining the influence of consumer choice on the material record (Crass and Brooks 1995). Ascertaining the influence of modernization and regional development on farms occupied during the recent past are also relevant research themes addressed in the archaeology of rural contexts (e.g., Groover 1992b; Cabak and Inkrot 1997; Cabak et al. 1999).

A Regionally Based Research Design for Farmstead Archaeology

The previously discussed research trends illustrate that farmstead archaeology has produced a substantial number of thorough studies. However, development of a holistic, regionally based research design for the topic would be beneficial and could serve to unify scholarship pertaining to the topic. The research design proposed in this study, which is potentially applicable to much of North America, contains two central elements. The first part consists of constructing a regional level historic context that is used for site interpretation. An interpretive context is created by defining important time periods within a culture history approach that allows identification of diachronic change and continuity, such as the colonial (ca. a.d. 1500 to 1790), antebellum (1790 to 1865), postbellum (1865 to 1900), and modern (1900 to 1950) periods. Constructing historic context also relies upon ideas in agricultural geography and is composed of identifying the agricultural production history of specific regions and placing study sites within this larger interpretive context. The second part of the research design involves constructing fine-grained site-specific analyses by combining extant detailed historic context with archaeological information. Elements of the suggested research design are drawn from several rural site studies (Groover 1992b, 1998, 2003, 2005; Cabak and Inkrot 1997; Cabak et al. 1999; Cabak and Groover 2004, 2006).

Effective site interpretation in historical archaeology relies upon reconstructing historic context. Historic context is used to address questions at different scales or levels of inquiry and refers to major trends that have influenced long-term historical development in different study regions. Historic context also consists of the basic cultural and historical details related to the past occupants of a site. Interpretive theory in history and the social sciences is also often used to construct context. For example, world systems theory, a body of ideas used in historical sociology (Wallerstein 1974, 1980, 1984, 1989), anthropology (Wolf 1982), and historical archaeology (Paynter 1982; South 1988) is a relevant starting point for crafting context in farmstead archaeology. World systems theorists maintain that commercial, profit-oriented economic activity is one of the strongest forces of development and change in the modern world—it fueled the discovery of the Americas and was subsequently a major catalyst of settlement and growth. This theoretical perspective looks at the long-term economic development of capitalism and the modern world during the past 500 years. In world systems theory, interpretive emphasis is placed upon the development of wealth and valuable commodities, such as agricultural products and industrial goods, and how the creation of these items has profoundly influenced the life experiences of households in different parts of the world. Farm households in the New World, especially those individuals that practiced commercial agriculture (or farming for profit) were significantly linked to the larger economic system that operated within farming communities. In turn, this economic system encompassed and connected, in a web-like manner, different regions of North America, including farming communities where crops were raised, small towns where farm products were marketed and shipped, and urban areas where farm goods were eventually consumed by non-food-producing households.

World systems theory provides a relevant overarching political-economic framework or structure for interpreting the larger topic of farmstead archaeology. The next step in assembling a research design for farmstead archaeology is to define important trends and time periods for different regions in North America. Contextual trends typical of many regions, for example, consist of culture contact situations between Native Americans and Old World groups, initial settlement of frontier areas by early farming households, the development of communities and the regional infrastructure, in addition to formalization of the economy, followed by articulation of study households with external markets and increasing consumerism. In archaeological research, these trends are usually reconstructed through reference to secondary studies by historians and are used to ground study sites within a specific historic context. These trends or research themes are also used to address several basic interpretive concerns, such as the primary function of a site (e.g., a farm residence, a gristmill, a blacksmith shop, a river landing), its role in the larger community and region, and how its primary function influenced the cultural and material experiences of the site's residents.

In addition to the trends that influenced the location and function of sites within larger cultural and economic systems, archaeologists are also interested in all of the specific cultural information related to a site that helps researchers understand the anthropological and historical experiences of the people who lived there. Crafting interpretive historic context relies upon seemingly mundane fragments of social history, such as the names of the sites' residents, their occupations, how long they lived at a site, household size and composition, and the residents' race, ethnicity, and religious affiliation. This kind of information provides ethnographic detail and imbues the archaeological record with cultural meaning. Without detailed historic and cultural context, the archaeological record is simply a static collection of old, discarded objects. At richly contextualized sites, or those residences that contain adequate historical documentation, the archaeological record is combined with abundant historical documentation and interpretive context to understand more effectively the lives of the sites' occupants. In the best situations, after detailed site studies have been completed, historical archaeologists often feel like they "know" the residents of a site the way they would be familiar with a friend or a living ethnographic study subject.

Historic context can also be constructed and used at multiple temporal and geographic scales of inquiry. Based upon concepts developed by French social historians in the *Annales* School (Braudel 1971, 1974, 1977, 1980, 1981) and ideas from the world systems perspective (Wallerstein 1974, 1980, 1984, 1989), quantitative historical context is especially useful for exploring material conditions at farmsteads. Fernand Braudel, the founder of the *Annales* School of French social historians, divided time into three main intervals: short-scale, medium-scale, and large-scale time. Short-scale time, the substance of standard history, focuses upon important events that transpired relatively rapidly within a few years, such as a war, the term of a president, or the drafting of an important political document, such as the U.S. Declaration of Independence. Medium-scale time encompasses the interval of decades or several lifetimes. Large-scale time, encompassing hundreds or thousands of years, is used to address long-term trends and the macroprocesses of history, such as the development and decline of specific societies or cultures. Large-scale time is also used to address geographic and environmental change.

The concept of medium-scale time is useful to farmstead archaeology (and historical archaeology in general) because it allows the identification of important cultural and historical processes. Cultural and historical processes are medium-term trends that substantially influenced and changed the everyday lives of people in the historic past, such as globalization and the discovery of the New World, the geographic and cultural intersections of different cultures, the development of capitalism and a global economy, the creation of industrialization and consumer culture, and the invention of new household technologies.

For farmstead archaeology studies, cultural and historical processes can be effectively reconstructed over medium-scale time through the use of quantitative-based historical records. Called serial history by the *Annales* School, the quantitative history of farms in the nation, the agricultural production history of a community or specific household, and the wealth holdings of an extended farm family over three generations are all valuable types of numerical context that help identify important contextual trends within a farm study. Consequently, the research design for rural archaeology presented in this chapter consists of reconstructing the agricultural production history and economic trends associated with regions, communities, and households and also investigating archaeologically how the primary agricultural activities associated with specific sites or farmsteads influenced daily living conditions.

Quantitative economic context is assembled from primary historical records. Economic information is used in turn to understand basic interpretive questions such as the crops grown at a farm, the degree of articulation within broader commercial systems, and whether a farm was a subsistence- or commercial-oriented operation. Quantitative information can also be used to determine if the study subjects at a site were raising more or fewer crops than their neighbors, the number of acres they farmed, and the kinds of household furnishings they used.

Several types of primary historical records, or those records created during the actual period of study, such as agricultural census records, tax records, deeds, and probate inventories, can help answer these questions. As summarized in Table 2.1, these records are used to reconstruct the agricultural and wealth-holding trends typical of a specific site and also a study region. For example, at sites occupied after 1850, the federal census of agriculture can be used to determine the types of products raised by a farm household. Through basic sampling methods (Groover 1998, 2003, 2005; Cabak and Groover 2004, 2006), agricultural census records taken from the neighbors surrounding a particular household can be used to define community-wide production characteristics. The households' agricultural production history can then be compared to look for similarities and differences in patterns of consumption. Probate inventories, a legal document describing the possessions of a person after death, can likewise be used to craft detailed quantitative information regarding household possessions and the standard of living practiced by a site's residents. This information can be a valuable tool in archaeological interpretation. For example, analysis of probate inventories can be used to reconstruct wealth-holding groups in a study region. The household possessions of a study subject can in turn be compared to the members of the surrounding community to understand better their standard of living.

Unfortunately, some types of historical information, such as the federal agricultural censuses, were only collected beginning in 1850, which excludes

Table 2.1. Examples of Primary Historical Records Used to Develop Archaeological Interpretive Context

Primary Records	Use
Land plat	Establish location of tracts and residences
Population census	Reconstruct household composition
Agricultural census	Establish crop production, acreage owned
Tax records	Identify real estate history of study subject
Will	Identify inheritance practices, wealth held at death
Probate inventory	Identify wealth held at death and household possessions
Portraits/sketches/photographs	Identify individuals and appearance of dwellings

much of the colonial and antebellum periods from consideration. Yet tax, landholding, and probate data usually exist for the pre-1850 periods in most regions, allowing reconstruction of wealth distributions and socioeconomic classes. In contrast to the frontier and antebellum periods, the period after 1850 possesses abundant documentary data, especially in the area of agricultural production.

Having reconstructed quantitative context via tax, landholding, probate inventory, and agricultural production data, specific sites that are being studied can be compared to the regionally and quantitatively based context to determine how economic activities at a particular site compared to the local community, surrounding region, and even larger nation. In turn, quantitative information can also be used to help better understand the material conditions and standard of living that site residents experienced, as revealed archaeologically.

Ideally, for a long-term research program or cultural resource management studies that have many significant sites that will be adversely impacted by proposed developments, sites that represent the entire range of households that resided in a specific physiographic region or study area should be sampled archaeologically. Research should be directed at reconstructing the complete diachronically based socioeconomic class structure of a defined area. One of the most manageable and socially meaningful units for this endeavor consists of sampling units within county tax districts, which approximate communities in the ethnographic sense. In turn, all of the tax districts in a county can be sampled followed by eventual investigation of several counties in the same physiographic region. This exercise allows intracounty and intercounty analyses for a given region. Also, several counties in different but adjacent physiographic regions can likewise be investigated in this manner, which can eventually result in a statewide synthesis of rural archaeological resources for different regions, such as the Southeast, Midwest, and Northeast.

Borrowing from classification typologies prevalent in agricultural geography (Anderson 1973; Tarrant 1974; Symons 1979), the full range of agricultural types by region can also be identified through primary documents, such as the agricultural census, and then systematically sampled archaeologically. For example, production types characteristic of the Ridge and Valley Province in East Tennessee during the nineteenth century are represented by yeoman or family-operated farms of various sizes that practiced mixed agriculture in addition to tenant farms, and a small minority of plantations and larger farms that relied on enslaved laborers. An archaeological study that attempts to systematically sample representative examples of all segments of a rural population through time, such as landowners of different landholding sizes, planters of different slaveholding and landowning sizes, and tenant farms of different sizes, would be useful in historical archaeology and would foster the development of a regional approach in the discipline (Groover 1998).

Several variables could be used for site selection, such as wealth groups (upper, middle, and lower wealth groups defined by quantitative interval from economic sample averages based on landholdings and personal property). Other relevant analysis variables include agricultural types of different acreage sizes, economic strategies, and production levels (plantations, subsistence and commercial farmsteads, and extractive-manufacturing works). Rural tenure types (owner-operators, tenants, and slaves); different racial groups (European Americans, African Americans, Native Americans, and multiracial households); and different family-gender types (nuclear, lineal, extended, and single-parent households) that existed between a defined time period or subperiod (such as the frontier period, 1780–1820, or the antebellum period, 1820–1865, etc.) are also important research topics.

In addition to creating a detailed historic context, the second part of the research design for farmstead archaeology consists of conducting fine-grained archaeological analyses of specific sites. Based upon the research trends discussed earlier, standard site topics typically addressed at farmsteads consist of identifying continuity and change in the domestic landscape and built environment over time, tracking architectural change, and examining the standard of living and material conditions experienced by farm households.

A useful and straightforward way of looking at farmsteads archaeologically is to view the farm as a material extension of the people who resided there. Farmsteads wax and wane with the life history of their residents. This is a seemingly simple idea, but it is an effective interpretive approach for better understanding cultural landscapes and material life at rural residences. For example, the domestic house lot that people create and inhabit is usually a dynamic material environment that changes over time with the life history of its occupants (Groover 2003). Consequently, reconstructing the life history of the domestic landscape at a site provides important insights about the people who lived there (Groover 2004).

Farm lots usually are either haphazardly arranged, called a strewn landscape pattern by cultural geographers (Jordan and Kaups 1989: 129–131) or are spatially preplanned and systematically organized, incorporating progressive ideas related to minimizing labor and maximizing production efficiency (McMurry 1988). The strewn pattern, typical of vernacular cultures in colonial and frontier situations, usually "grows" organically or in an unplanned manner over time as the farm household matures. In contrast, spatially preplanned farm lots became prevalent during the 1800s as commercial agriculture and the ideology of progressive farming emerged in different regions (McMurry 1988; Sayers and Nassaney 1999). Reconstructing site structure and the spatial characteristics of a house or farm lot at a site that does not possess standing structures involves the archaeological identification of the subsurface locations and related functions of outbuildings and other improvements. Farms with different types of crop and livestock regimes would likely possess different types and arrangements of outbuildings. For example, the farm lot at an early 1800s pioneer mixed grain and livestock farm in the Midwest would be different than a late 1800s commercial dairy farm, with large milking barns and livestock pens.

In addition to landscape change, architectural change is also an important topic in farmstead archaeology that can be incorporated into research designs. Similar to house lots, early colonial and frontier houses, such as log cabins, post-in-the-ground structures, or wattle and daub dwellings, were vernacular or folk structures that potentially reflect the culture, ethnicity, race, and place of origin of their inhabitants. Conversely, as popular culture, consumerism, and the commercial economy developed in different regions, some (but not all) households began adopting national style dwellings. These new styles of dwellings were often advertised in catalogs and other popular publications that illustrated floor plans and the exteriors of the houses. House plan catalogs during the 1800s are similar to house plan books and catalogs available in our own time. National and academic style dwellings, such as Georgian, Greek Revival, Italianate, or Victorian styles, typically appear first among affluent households and over time were adopted by larger segments of the rural population. In many situations, vernacular style dwellings were renovated and updated by adding national style embellishments to them. Through this process, the residents of modest dwellings incorporated national style elements into the fabric of their residences. Tracking the geographic, temporal, and social spread of national dwelling styles is a relevant topic at farmstead sites.

Besides dwelling style, which is indicative of national-level influences, the life history of houses also often reflects the long-term history of their occupants. As farm households grow and mature over time, dwellings often experience expansion and renovation episodes that reflect this shared history. Through careful dating of architectural features and archaeological deposits, architectural and landscape site events, such as the addition of a kitchen ell or side pen on a log house, can be linked chronologically to specific households. When combined, the sequence of landscape and site events defined archaeologically reveals the long-term changes that occurred at a site (e.g., Groover 1998, 2003).

Beyond architectural questions, archaeologists are also interested in identifying the standard of living and material conditions experienced by a farm household. The archaeological record is particularly important for addressing this topic and is used to determine the kinds of household furnishings the residents used, the types of food they ate, and the extent to which their standard of living was influenced by consumer trends and popular culture.

In summary, the proposed research design for farmstead archaeology involves creating detailed interpretive context for a region, study area, and specific farm households. The material culture recovered from the archaeological record at farm sites is then placed within this larger interpretive context. In some situations, the archaeological record will agree with the documentary record and provide greater interpretive detail than the historical record regarding diet, foodways, and the household standard of living. In other instances, documentary and archaeological information will disagree with one another, suggesting that unidentified cultural reasons are responsible for the identified lack of agreement between written and archaeological information sources. In the best situations, the combination of primary records and archaeological data results in greater understanding of the site and its inhabitants—greater understanding than can be achieved by merely relying upon documents or artifacts by themselves (Little 1994).

Evaluating the Site Significance of Farmsteads

During the past century the federal government has enacted a suite of preservation laws, such as the Antiquities Act of 1906, the Historic Sites Act of
1935, and the National Historic Preservation Act of 1966, that are designed
to protect historical, cultural, and archaeological resources (Hardesty and
Little 2000: 7–9). Several preservation laws were created to protect archaeological sites located on federally managed land, such as National Parks,
National Forests, and military bases. Archaeological preservation laws are
also designed to protect sites that might be impacted by federally funded
development initiatives, such as highway construction projects. Preservation laws created a conservation orientation in American archaeology often
referred to as a type of cultural resource management studies (CRM). Most
archaeologists in the United States today are employed in cultural resource
management.

Archaeologists conducting cultural resource management studies are
charged with identifying archaeological sites, evaluating their significance
according to National Register eligibility criteria created in the National
Historic Preservation Act of 1966, and providing archaeological recommen-
dations to land managers, state archaeologists, and clients regarding which
sites will experience adverse impact by earth-disturbing development projects, such as a road or building construction projects.

CRM studies typically consist of archaeological site survey, site testing,
and archaeological data recovery excavations. Archaeological site surveys
are conducted to create a basic inventory of archaeological sites in a specific
study area, such as sites located in the footprint of a new highway or the
flood pool of a dam. During site survey, archaeologists identify the location, size, and period of occupation of specific sites and create an overall site
inventory for the archaeological project area. Following site survey, site testing occurs in which exploratory archaeological excavations are conducted.
The purpose of site testing is to obtain more detailed information about
a site and further evaluate its research importance. It is at this step in the
CRM process that archaeologists determine if a site can provide important
information about our national patrimony. Questions addressed during
site testing consist mainly of the condition of the archaeological deposits,
whether they are disturbed or largely undisturbed and intact, the amount
of artifacts at the site, and the time periods when a site was occupied. If the
archaeological deposits at a site are well preserved and the site has relatively
abundant amounts of artifacts, then the site could be evaluated as possess-

ing research potential. The information value of a site is mainly determined through reference to Criterion D of the National Register of Historic Places, which states that a site may be deemed archaeologically significant if it can contribute important information to a specific research topic. In contrast, if a site cannot contribute relevant information to a research topic, then its archaeological value would be considered limited.

After site testing is conducted, those sites that possess intact and relatively abundant deposits are further evaluated using an important concept in cultural resource management studies called *site significance*. At a fundamental level, site significance is used by archaeologists to evaluate whether specific archaeological sites should be preserved or destroyed, based on Criterion D of the National Register of Historic Places. The concept is also used to formulate specific research questions that in turn establish the research value of a specific site. If a site is deemed to have research potential that can help answer important archaeological questions, then it is evaluated as having archaeological research significance. Ideally, archaeologically significant sites should be preserved and viewed as a finite cultural resource that, once destroyed or excavated, cannot be replaced. Unfortunately, in many situations, adverse impacts to significant archaeological sites cannot be avoided, resulting in the eventual destruction of the site. When this situation occurs, the adverse impact to significant sites is mitigated through data-recovery archaeological excavations. During such excavations, significant sites are entirely excavated or portions of a site are excavated to recover important information about the site before it is destroyed. After the fieldwork is completed, the results of data-recovery excavations are summarized in technical documents called site excavation reports that present the findings of the excavation projects. In the best situations, the findings from data-recovery projects are also eventually disseminated to the archaeological community and interested public via conference papers, journal articles, books, magazine articles, and video programs.

As the different stages of fieldwork conducted in cultural resource management studies illustrate, the concept of site significance is important, since it is used to determine if a site will be destroyed or preserved or become the subject of data-recovery excavations. Consequently, archaeological research significance is based on several interrelated factors. Most important, site significance involves determining whether a site can contribute important archaeological information to the current state of knowledge related to specific research topics. The condition and preservation of the archaeological record at a specific site also influence significance.

Regarding farmstead studies (and other archaeological research topics), the current state of knowledge depends upon researchers periodically reviewing and summarizing what is currently known and not known about a specific topic. Called a synthesis, these periodic reviews are crucial in CRM; they help summarize existing knowledge and provide new research questions for future studies. Today, many state preservation agencies in America have planning and management documents that provide historic contexts for archaeological research. To help determine site significance, these documents summarize the current state of archaeological knowledge for specific time periods and identify well-developed research topics or knowledge areas and topics that require further research effort.

Defining the archaeological significance and research potential of farm sites depends upon several related factors: primarily a well-defined historic context for a specific study region and a current and continuously updated summary of the current state of knowledge related to the topic. In addition to these two elements, new ideas presented in books, journal articles, technical reports, and conference presentations should also be incorporated into ongoing research in specific regions.

Establishing a historic context for a study region primarily involves defining research topics and themes that guide inquiry. The themes are determined by drawing upon the particular historical trends that transpired in a study region. For example, in the American Midwest, the history of rural life can be divided into the early historic period (ca. 1600s–1700s), the federal/antebellum period (ca. 1800–1860s), and the postbellum/modern period (ca. 1860s–1950). Examples of important research topics and themes for the early historic period are historic Native American communities, forts and traders, early settler households, early commercial farming, and infrastructure development, such as the creation of roads, river landings, rural communities, and processing facilities (e.g., gristmills and sawmills). Examples of relevant research themes for the federal/antebellum and postbellum/modern periods are the transition from subsistence to commercial farming, farm modernization/mechanization, and how these larger trends influenced the built environment, domestic landscape, and household material culture at farms. Other important topics for these time periods include infrastructure development, such as the creation of canals, railroads, and railroad communities.

As might be expected, subtopics or supporting research questions can also be further defined for primary topics in each of the culture history periods. For example, important study topics that could be addressed relevant to Native American communities are represented by the extent of cultural continuity and change revealed archaeologically, the timing and extent of participation in commercial economies, and issues related to ethnogenesis, acculturation, cultural interaction, cultural resistance, and cultural maintenance. For sites occupied by early settler households, topics related to cultural adaptation, cultural restructuring, the persistence and demise of ethnically based material traditions, and the transition from subsistence to commercial economies would also be relevant research questions.

Once a detailed research design has been crafted that includes specific research themes, topics, and research questions, then preexisting archaeological studies can be placed in this framework to establish the current state of knowledge pertaining to different topics. As new sites are encountered, then this preexisting framework can be used to evaluate site significance. For example, in many parts of the United States, little is known archaeologically about settler households, so their mere absence in the archaeological literature of a state or region underscores their archaeological importance and significance as an archaeological information resource. Consequently, when well-preserved settler sites are discovered, they can be considered significant since little is known about these archaeological resources in many regions of the country.

As mentioned, a long-range goal of this suggested research strategy is to assemble information about different research themes for specific physiographic regions. Detailed intraregional studies could be used to define economic and material characteristics for a specific area among different economic classes and site types. Eventually, compatible information could be assembled by different researchers that would allow comparison of different agricultural production areas in the United States. For example, if information was available, material comparisons based on archaeological data could be conducted between grain and livestock farms in East Tennessee, tobacco farms in Middle Tennessee, farms of the Cotton Belt in the Lower South, grain and livestock farms in the Midwest, and wheat farms in the Great Plains. A research strategy of this extent has the potential of eventually producing a synthesis of rural archaeology and material life for the entire nation, or at least it could address the major economic-production types prevalent in North America. The implementation of this type of research framework has been previously proposed for rural site studies in the Savannah River valley (Cabak and Inkrot 1997; Cabak et al. 1999) and East Tennessee (Groover 1998). A research design of this nature is particularly relevant for creating a regional context and placing sites in a broadly conceived analytical format in which variables related to rural production types, socioeconomic class, standard of living, and the built environment are quickly identified and controlled for.

Concerning the practical relevance of this outlined research strategy, an approach that creates a quantitatively based historic context is especially applicable to evaluating and managing cultural resources within specific regions. This geographic scale or situation, which at first consideration might seem unrealistic or unmanageable, is typical of most public land reserves, such as national forests, military bases, and federally created reservoirs. Consequently, an appreciable amount of site-level information already exists in many parts of the United States, and the next step would be for different researchers to begin assembling existing archaeological information into a standardized and comparable format. The long-term purpose of this effort would be to synthesize existing archaeological information to understand better the material basis of rural life in the United States and consequently better preserve and manage our existing resources pertaining to farmstead archaeology.

3

Colonial Farmsteads

The cultural-historical process of colonization was set in motion with the discovery of the New World in the late 1400s. During this time people from the Old World, notably Europeans and Africans, came in sustained contact with Native Americans. An important topic in historical archaeology that is explored through primary historical records and material culture, the colonial period in the United States dates from the 1500s to the late 1700s. During the colonial era, farmsteads were an important type of settlement established by Europeans in North America. The archaeology of colonial farmsteads is characterized by several important research themes. The extent that settlers attempted to replicate Old World cultural conditions is an important archaeological issue. Consequently, migration, adaptation, simplification, and restructuring are prominent questions addressed in colonial archaeology. Called cultural continuity by archaeologists, in some situations settlers attempted to consciously maintain their cultural practices and ideologies. In many other locations, settlers entered the New World but did not endure the experience unchanged. As a result, the extent and nature of cultural continuity, change, and transformation that colonial settlers experienced are prevalent questions addressed by historical archaeologists.

In addition to the basic transformative effect of the colonial frontier upon settlers, a major cultural transition also occurred between the 1500s and 1900s that is an important subject in archaeological studies. Beginning in the 1700s, cultures in North America experienced the transition from a premodern, preindustrial way of life to a modern, industrially based society. This event is important archaeologically because it has influenced the material culture used by people in the historic past in profound ways. Preindustrial people in North America are often called vernacular or folk cultures (Deetz 1977). Living along the North American colonial frontier in different locations, such as New England, the Mid-Atlantic region, the coastal Southeast, and the major rivers of the Midwest, these folk cultures from the Old World were organized by the concept of tradition in which cultural practices were maintained over relatively long periods of time. Cultural traditions are rules that determine what is considered the appropriate or right way of doing things.

Since these societies existed before industrialization, colonial-period folk cultures in North America were self-sufficient, meaning that they had to be able to take care of themselves in order to survive. Farming households during the colonial period are good examples of self-sufficient vernacular cultures. Their place of origin in the Old World (their nationality), their ethnicity (or cultural identity), and their related cultural customs often determined where they settled, how they arranged their farms spatially, what kinds of houses they built and lived in, what kinds of crops and livestock they raised, what kinds of foods they ate, and the types of household goods they used. Fortunately for archaeologists, these vernacular-based cultural practices often had a strong material basis and can sometimes (in ideal situations) be identified archaeologically, such as by the style or floor plan of a house or the specific kinds of pottery used by farm families.

These regionally based vernacular societies adjusted to New World conditions, and by the first half of the 1700s the first stirrings of industrialization—an incredibly profound source of social change—began in Europe. Industrialization among colonial residents in the New World at first had fairly subtle implications: ceramic tableware, such as plates, bowls, and mugs, began to be mass produced in some of the world's first pottery factories in England. Likewise, hardware for firearms was eventually manufactured through standardized production in the late 1700s and early 1800s. Only after the second half of the 1800s does the full brunt of industrialization become fully apparent in the archaeological record, with a substantial increase in household items and material deposition, such as container glass and personal artifacts, at most domestic sites.

Although the archaeological implications of industrialization are relatively imperceptible at many colonial sites, industrialization nonetheless set in motion and was accompanied by the development of consumerism and popular culture, which eventually exerted profound influence upon most households in America. Many aspects of consumerism and popular culture began with the upper classes in North America during the colonial period. Consumer goods were used as status objects to set their owners apart from lower and middle segments of colonial society. Popular consumer culture influenced many aspects of daily life: domestic architecture, landscape design, domestic furnishings, dress, and foodways (Deetz 1977). On colonial farms, archaeologists often explore the maintenance of traditional culture and attempt to identify the initial penetration and origins of consumer culture in rural contexts.

From Landless Farmer to Propertied Planter: The Archaeology of Rural Upward Mobility at the William Strickland Site

The discovery of the New World offered the possibility of a better life for many Old World settlers. Attracted by the prospects of inexpensive land, economic security, and greater social freedom, farming households began settling the Atlantic coast of North America initially in the 1600s and then in greater numbers during the 1700s. Today, citizens of the United States take pride in the American dream that originated in the country's colonial past—the potential for improvement and success through hard work.

Historically, many farm families experienced the transition from being landless tenant farmers to owning their own land and prosperous farms. A rural household's socioeconomic position was often determined by their relationship to the land they worked. This system of social rank was called the agricultural ladder (Stine 1989, 1990). For example, during the colonial period many individuals came to America as indentured servants, in which case a sponsor paid their passage in return for a period of servitude. Once they arrived in North America, many indentured servants became tenant farmers and farmed land that they did not own for several years while they worked to repay their debt of passage. Over time, many farm families that did not own land were eventually able to become landowning farmers and improve their economic situation. However, a recent study of the agricultural ladder during the late 1800s and early 1900s indicates that rural class mobility among farm families was often very difficult (Alston and Ferrie 2005). The William Strickland site (Grettler et al. 1991; Catts et al. 1995) in central Delaware illustrates one colonial success story, in which a landless farmer over time was able to become a prosperous landowner.

The William Strickland site is located on the Eastern Shore of central Delaware, along the Lower Coastal Plain (Figure 1.2). During the 1720s, small and middling farmers began migrating from the Chesapeake, such as the Eastern Shore of Maryland, into central Delaware, which was characterized by fertile sandy soils and tidal marshes. The William Strickland site, located in Smyrna on Duck Creek Hundred, Kent County, was occupied from the late 1600s to the late 1700s. Members of the William Strickland family were the primary occupants of the site between ca. 1726 to 1764. During this approximately 40-year interval, William Strickland rose from the ranks of landless tenants to become a propertied farmer. In the 1726 tax lists, the earliest record of Strickland in Duck Creek Hundred, he was among the lower 50 percent of wealth holders that held 25 percent of the wealth in the community. Conversely, 25 years later during the mid-eighteenth century, he was among the top 10 percent of taxed households.

William Strickland achieved colonial upward mobility through a land grant and a successful strategy of mixed grain and livestock farming. His family during the middle 1700s consisted of his second wife, Rachel, his older daughters Rebecca and Elizabeth from his first marriage, and an infant daughter, Rachel, from his second marriage. Three adult slaves, Boston, Andrew, and Nan, also lived at the farm. The Strickland household members and slaves worked a 223-acre tract of land, raising cattle, sheep, and pigs. They also grew wheat, rye, oats, and corn. Although William Strickland owned a small number of slaves, he is a relevant example of a slave-holding farmer rather than a planter.

Paralleling livestock herding at the Strickland site, during the colonial period, the raising of livestock was a lucrative farming activity in frontier regions, as Old World residents brought husbandry knowledge from such parts of Western Europe as Britain and Ireland. Enslaved Africans also often had extensive knowledge of livestock farming. Herding was a cost-effective farming practice, since it did not require the labor investment needed to clear and plant new fields, typical of settler agriculture. Further, Atlantic coastal areas with sandy soils and tidal marsh environments were often not well suited for farming but were ideal for the raising of livestock using the open range system, in which branded stock animals foraged over large open areas. Many small fortunes were made by colonial livestock raisers, and herds of between 50 to 100 head were common (Brooks et al. 2000; Groover and Brooks 2003). Shortly after his death, 55 head of livestock were listed in William Strickland's probate inventory in 1754—23 sheep, 15 hogs, 12 cows, 4 calves, and 1 bull—representing a relatively substantial herd size, suggesting that the raising of livestock was an important activity at the site.

The William Strickland farm was discovered in 1990 by personnel with the University of Delaware Center for Archaeological Research (UDCAR) during an archaeological survey of a proposed road improvement project, the State Route 1 Corridor (Grettler et al. 1991; Catts et al. 1995). As part of the State Route 1 Corridor project conducted for the Delaware Department of Transportation, staff persons with the Center for Archaeological

Research located the Strickland site and conducted site testing at the colonial farmstead. Based on the results of site testing, the Strickland farmstead was considered to be archaeologically significant and an important cultural resource. The archaeological deposits at the site were well preserved, and it was deemed likely that the site could provide valuable information about colonial life in the region. Consequently, data-recovery investigations were conducted to preserve the archaeological information at the Strickland site. If site excavations had not been conducted, important archaeological information at the farm would have been destroyed or otherwise lost in the wake of the proposed transportation improvement project.

The site investigations conducted at the William Strickland farmstead aptly illustrate cultural resource management (CRM) studies that are routinely conducted by archaeologists in the United States. Required by federal and state laws, CRM studies are one of the main ways that archaeology is conducted in America (Hardesty and Little 2000). These studies are intended to help manage and preserve archaeological sites threatened by earth-disturbing development projects. If archaeological sites discovered during CRM studies cannot be protected from proposed projects, such as road construction in the case of the Strickland site, then the site is excavated as part of an archaeological data-recovery project. These projects often result in the excavation of large spatial areas, such as 100-by-100-foot excavation blocks. Large excavation areas are required to reveal the layout and spatial organization of the site—the former location of structures, fence lines, and activity areas. Large samples of artifacts are also recovered from data-recovery excavations. These artifacts help historical archaeologists reconstruct the characteristics of daily life during the recent past at different sites.

The William Strickland site was considered to be an important archaeological resource for several reasons. First, initial fieldwork determined that the site contained undisturbed archaeological deposits beneath the plowed topsoil at the site, called the plowzone. After the field investigators had determined that the site contained intact deposits, they immediately knew it was an important cultural resource, because few eighteenth-century colonial farmsteads had been previously studied archaeologically in Delaware. Consequently, the Strickland farm was a rare example of a type of site that had not been well documented through archaeology. Further, the State of Delaware relies upon a State Management Plan (De Cunzo and Catts 1990; De Cunzo 2004) that helps archaeologists effectively evaluate the research value of archaeological sites, based upon a detailed research framework. The state management plan helped further evaluate the research value of the Strickland site and highlighted its importance.

Within the Delaware Management Plan, the Strickland farm corresponds to the period of Intensified and Durable Occupation in the history of the state. Important research topics relating to this period discussed in the state management plan are domestic life and rural economy. As a result, the site investigators argued that the Strickland farm was archaeologically significant as a research information source since it could help answer a number of important questions related to domestic life, rural economy, and the farm landscape in colonial Delaware.

The research topics of domestic life and rural economy refer to family and household activities related to economic production and material consumption. Simply put, the study of domestic life and household economy often centers upon how a household made a living and what types of household goods and furnishings they used. The number of people in a household, their ages, occupations, and consumer activities, are also important archaeological questions related to domestic life. For farmstead studies, the types of agricultural products raised by a household and whether they were involved in commercial production are also important questions that would have influenced the material conditions that a rural family experienced.

The characteristics of the domestic landscape that a household inhabited and how it changed or remained the same over time are also important questions within the management plan used by archaeologists in Delaware. The Strickland farm was considered to be archaeologically important because it could help answer questions related to the layout and spatial arrangement of colonial farms and the types of dwellings and outbuildings that settlers used. For the colonial period in the United States, archaeology is often the main information source available for exploring topics related to the daily life of early settlers and the domestic landscape they built and inhabited.

In addition to primary research questions related to domestic life and the farm landscape, archaeologists who investigated the Strickland site were also interested in addressing questions about the basic characteristics of daily life at the colonial farm. What kinds of food did the settlers eat? What types of household furnishings did they use? Did they have access to popular consumer goods of the time, or did they experience the austere living conditions typically associated with the American colonial frontier? Further, the site investigators also emphasized that, in general, the Strickland farm could help illustrate the transition from frontier conditions to settled life that occurred in Delaware between the 1730s and 1770s. Again, this is an important period of change in American history, especially for settlements along the Atlantic coast, and much of the information related to this time period includes artifacts and other fragments of daily life preserved at archaeological sites.

Data-recovery excavations conducted at the William Strickland site, located in a cultivated field, included sampling the plowzone through the excavation of archaeological units and subsequent mechanical site stripping. These efforts revealed a substantial amount of information about rural life in colonial Delaware. The Strickland farm consisted of a square enclosed work yard formed by buildings and fence lines (Figure 3.1). The farm lot contained a post-in-the-ground dwelling and a post-in-the-ground detached kitchen (Figure 3.2). Post-in-the-ground dwellings, also called earthfast structures, were built by colonists digging postholes and seating the wooden timber wall supports of the structures in the postholes (Carson et al. 1988). Documented at colonial sites from Maine to Florida, earthfast construction was an affordable, expedient, and widely used method of erecting dwellings and outbuildings along the eastern frontier. In addition to the two earthfast structures, excavations also revealed that the Strickland site contained the remains of a smokehouse with a cellar, two outbuildings, two wells, refuse disposal areas, called sheet midden, fence lines, and a daub pit or partially complete cellar hole.

The recovery of 19,000 artifacts and 8,000 animal bone fragments helped reconstruct economic activities, daily material conditions, and the standard of living experienced by the Strickland family. Typical of colonial domestic sites, the majority of the artifacts recovered from the Strickland farmstead were related to foodways and architecture. The remaining artifacts, occurring in small numbers, were associated with household items and personal possessions.

A useful way of looking at colonial artifact assemblages is to sort them by primary consumption-related artifacts and secondary artifacts. Primary consumption artifacts, as the name implies, are items and resources that were used in large amounts for a short period of time and then were discarded, quickly becoming part of the archaeological record. For colonial contexts, primary consumption items were mainly foodways-related artifacts, especially animal bones from meals, ceramics used in the kitchen during meal preparation, and ceramics such as tableware used during the consumption of meals.

Secondary artifacts are consumer items that occur in small amounts

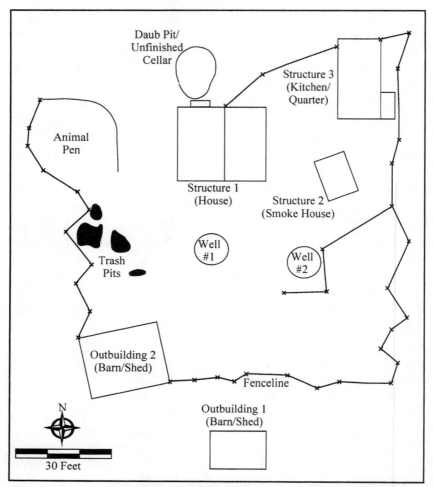

Figure 3.1. Site map of the William Strickland farm. By permission of Delaware Department of Transportation, from Catts et al. 1995, Figure 47.

and are related to personal possessions and household furnishings. Such artifacts have a longer use-life and often enter the archaeological record through accidental loss rather than intentional discard. Architectural artifacts, such as nails, are not included in these analysis categories or the following artifact discussion since architectural items were relatively static artifacts—they were placed in the fabric of a dwelling or structure and then rarely used further. Architectural items were also not discarded and depos-

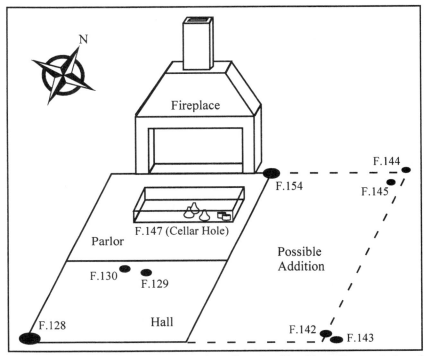

Figure 3.2. Plan map of the dwelling at the William Strickland farm. By permission of Delaware Department of Transportation, from Catts et al. 1995, Figure 15.

ited into the archaeological record until the structure was actually modified or destroyed.

Artifacts related to primary consumption activities at the site comprise 98.85 percent of the artifact assemblage (excluding architectural items as mentioned previously). Conversely, secondary artifacts represent a mere 1.15 percent of the assemblage. Considered in more detail (Table 3.1), the primary consumption-related items consist of foodways artifacts, especially faunal remains, ceramics, kitchen utensils, and glass items. Tobacco pipe fragments, another type of primary consumption artifact, were also abundantly represented at the site. This distribution of objects at the site clearly illustrates that discarded artifacts were mainly associated with food, and few personal possessions or household furnishings were discarded or recovered archaeologically.

Animal bones from the site, the largest artifact category, reveal important information about frontier diet in colonial Delaware. Eighty-nine percent

Table 3.1. Distribution of the Primary Consumption-Related Artifacts and Secondary Artifacts Recovered from the William Strickland Farm

Primary Consumption	%	n
Artifact Categories		
Faunal	87.00	7,758
Ceramics	2.50	222
Glass items	0.50	35
Tobacco pipes	10.00	925
Consumption total	100.00	8,940
Secondary Artifacts		
Clothing	59.00	62
Arms	14.00	15
Medical	7.00	7
Household	5.00	5
Personal	4.00	4
Farming	11.00	11
Secondary artifacts total	100.00	104
Cons. related artifacts total	98.85	8,940
Secondary artifacts total	1.15	104
Total artifacts	100.00	9,044

(n=2,383) of the identified animal bones consisted of domesticated species, and 11 percent (n=293) were wild species. Paralleling the livestock listed in William Strickland's 1754 probate inventory, domesticated animals used for food at the farm consisted of pig, cow, sheep, and chicken. Pork was the predominant domesticated meat consumed. A small amount of wild foods used to supplement meals included water animals (catfish, perch, turtle, and crab), mammals (deer, squirrel, opossum, rabbit, and raccoon), and fowl (goose and duck).

The foodways artifacts recovered from the William Strickland site aptly illustrate the types of items typically recovered from colonial farmsteads. Ceramics, glass items, and kitchen utensils are the main manufactured foodways artifacts recovered. Ceramics were used for either processing and storing foodstuffs or preparing and consuming meals. Ceramics from the Strickland site were placed in several analysis categories, consisting of ceramic type and ceramic function. The ceramic type category consisted of specific ware types. The ceramic functional category was composed of hollowware and flatware and specific vessel forms, such as plates, bowls, teacups, and mugs.

The ceramics from the Strickland site were summarized using a method called minimum number of ceramic vessel analysis (mncv), a conservative method of estimating the number of ceramic vessels present in an archaeo-logically recovered sample. Minimum vessel counts are typically based on a single vessel attribute, such as vessel rims. All of the identical plate rims with the same transfer-printed decoration pattern, for example, would be grouped together during mncv analysis. All of the similar sherds would then be considered to represent one single vessel. Minimum vessel counts are a conservative way of estimating vessels in a ceramic sample. Historical archaeologists also use ceramic sherd counts as a less conservative method of describing the characteristics of ceramic samples.

Redware vessels comprised 54 percent of the ceramic vessels recovered from the Strickland site (n=127 minimum number of ceramic vessels). Redware was a prevalent ceramic in North America between the 1500s and 1800s. Usually manufactured locally, it typically exhibits a paste or vessel body color ranging from red to tan. Redware vessels were glazed with lead, usually only on the interior of vessels. They were often used to process and store dairy products during the colonial period.

In addition to redware, a broad range of other ceramic types was also recovered from the site, consisting of stoneware (17 percent, n=40 mncv), tin-glazed earthenware (9 percent, n=22 mncv), Staffordshire (6 percent, n=15 mncv), porcelain (4 percent, n=10 mncv), and several wares in small proportions (10 percent, n=23 mncv), such as Buckley ware, agate ware, North Devon gravel tempered ware, and Whieldon (Figure 3.3).

Analysis of ceramics by form illustrates the foodways practiced at the Strickland farm and the range of vessel types used by the farm family. Ce-ramics are often placed in the analysis categories of hollowware and flatware. Hollowware vessels, such as bowls, pitchers, and jugs, were used as food and beverage vessels during meals and as storage containers. Conversely, flat ware forms, such as plates, were used for food consumption. The propor-tion of hollow- and flatware sherds from a site indicates whether the site residents were consuming meals mainly from bowls, typical of vernacular or folk foodways such as stews and soups, or whether they were using plates and portioned servings, food consumption practices that are characteristic of more modern foodways (Deetz 1977).

A total of 38 serving bowls were identified at the Strickland farm com-pared to 26 plates. Hollowware comprised 59 percent of the vessel distribu-tion as opposed to flatware that represented 41 percent of the hollowware-flatware sample. Put another way, the ceramics from the site exhibit a 3-to-2 hollowware to flatware ratio, suggesting that both vernacular-based food-ways focusing on stews and soups were consumed at the site along with

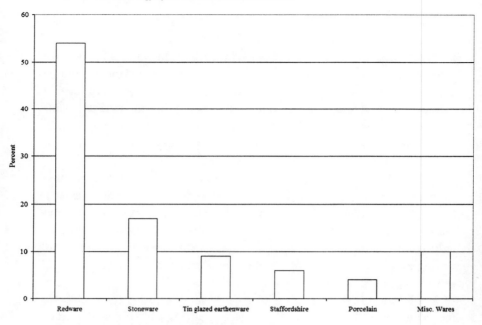

Figure 3.3. Distribution of ceramics by ware at the William Strickland farm.

a slightly lower prevalence of portioned meals from plates. It should also be noted that pewter tableware was listed in William Strickland's probate inventory, and these vessels more than likely were plates, which would suggest that an equal amount of hollowware and flatware was used by the household during different meals. In summary, the hollowware to flatware results indicate that foodways were certainly in transition at this colonial farm, from folk to modern practices, as would be expected during this period.

An additional way to reconstruct foodways from archaeologically recovered ceramic fragments is to categorize the identified vessel forms by functional categories. When the ceramic data from the Strickland farm are organized by functionally based vessel categories, several informative trends are apparent (Figure 3.4). Food consumption vessels (32 percent of the mncv) are the most prevalent functional category represented in the recovered ceramic assemblage, followed by beverage containers (28 percent of the mncv), food preparation and service vessels (21 percent), and food storage ceramics (19 percent).

Regarding food consumption forms, as discussed above, a slightly larger proportion of bowls and related hollowwares were used by the site residents (59 percent of the mncv), consisting of serving bowls, posset cups, porrin-

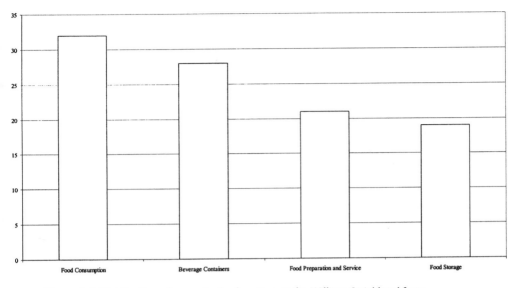

Figure 3.4. Distribution of ceramics by function at the William Strickland farm.

gers, and mush cups. Redware bowls predominate in the bowl vessel count, followed by tin-glazed, white salt–glazed stoneware, Staffordshire, and Whieldon ware. Twenty-six plates were also identified in the assemblage, representing the remaining 41 percent of the vessels in the food consumption analysis category by minimum vessel count. The plates were mainly manufactured from redware, but tin-glazed, white salt–glazed, and Staffordshire examples were also present in smaller amounts.

Ceramics used for beverage consumption are the second most prevalent vessel forms at the site. Twenty-five mugs were identified in the minimum vessel count, followed by tea cups (n=19 mncv), saucers (n=10), and teapots (n=3). White salt–glazed vessels were the most prevalent in the teaware assemblage, followed by porcelain and tin-glazed earthenware vessels.

Tea was not merely a fashionable beverage during the eighteenth century but was part of popular culture and social ritual that was used to denote class membership. In addition to the teaware recovered archaeologically from the site, William Strickland's inventory likewise listed a broad range of additional tea service and equipage, such as six silver teaspoons, a tea table, teaware, a tea kettle, and some old silver. Despite their frontier setting, the Strickland family was apparently concerned with properly entertaining guests at their residence.

Food preparation and service vessels comprise 21 percent of the minimum vessel count, consisting of pitchers, bowls, serving dishes, and platters. These vessels were used to prepare and serve foods during meals. Redware vessels were the predominant ware type in this category, followed by Buckley ware, agate ware, white salt–glazed stoneware, Nottingham, and English brown stoneware.

Last, food storage containers represent 19 percent of the total minimum vessel count identified at the Strickland farm. These vessels are represented by milk pans, butter pots, and jars. The container vessels were mainly made of redware and stoneware to a lesser extent. Redware vessels used for dairying consist of 21 milk pans, which are large bowls used to process milk, 11 butter pots, which are large, crock-like vessels used to store butter, and 3 jars. The redware storage vessels are important because they can be linked directly to dairying and agricultural activities conducted at the site. Based on the large number of dairying vessels (n=35) identified at the Strickland farm, they are also important material indicators of the commercial dairying that occurred at the farm.

Besides the ceramics recovered from the Strickland farm, other primary consumption-related artifacts include a small number of fragments from glassware, several kitchen utensils, and a large number of tobacco pipe fragments. Glass pieces from the excavation indicate the Strickland family used stemmed wine glasses, tumblers, and glass table vessels. They likewise consumed wine, indicated by the recovery of wine bottle fragments. A relatively large sample of metal kitchen utensils—spoons, forks, and knives—was also recovered.

In addition to foodways items, artifacts with short use-life related to leisure time and relaxation are illustrated by a large number of clay tobacco pipe fragments. The tobacco pipe fragments comprise 76 percent of the primary consumption-related artifacts, indicating pipe smoking was a frequent activity at the farm.

In contrast to primary consumption-related artifacts, secondary artifacts, consisting of personal possessions and household furnishings, represent a mere 1 percent of the items (n=104) recovered from the Strickland farm. These artifacts are associated with clothing manufacture and maintenance (straight pins, buttons, scissors, and a thimble), personal possessions (pocket knives, a straight razor, and medicine bottle fragments), household items consisting of several keys and padlock parts, several gunflints for firearms, and several farm tool fragments.

Considered together, the primary consumption-related artifacts, when combined with the existing probate inventory, reveal a great amount of detail concerning rural foodways and daily material life at the Strickland farm during the middle of the eighteenth century. The farm family consumed mainly pork and predominantly used locally made redware vessels. The family also ate liquid-based meals from bowls and consumed portioned meals from plates in equal prevalence. The family was apparently aware of popular dining practices, as indicated by six dining chairs listed in William Strickland's probate inventory. During meals they consumed wine and other alcoholic beverages. Family members also enjoyed drinking tea and had a noticeable amount of tea paraphernalia and tea-related furnishings. After meals and during other daily activities, the adult members of the family also enjoyed tobacco smoked in clay pipes.

The Strickland site is archaeologically compelling because it aptly illustrates that early colonial consumerism in frontier settings focused mainly upon food-related activities. Consequently, colonial consumerism, based on the results of archaeology, began first in the domain of food preparation and consumption in households. Consumerism later spread to other areas of household life. Part of this early, food-based consumerism during the colonial period was strictly utilitarian—farm families needed mundane, inexpensive storage containers such as redware and stoneware vessels to conduct daily tasks, such as dairying. Likewise, the processing and preparation of meals also depended upon the use of socially invisible foodways artifacts, such as large redware bowls and platters.

However, when socially visible artifacts related to foodways are considered, these items take on an entirely different role in the household compared to mundane foodways objects. Expensive pewter dishes, stemmed wine glasses, and matching teaware were used to communicate social position and fashion sense to dinner guests at the Strickland farm, and these items were used by the farm residents to reinforce the idea that they were aware of and actively participated in larger popular trends during the colonial period. These items also become even more important when the upward mobility of the farm family is considered: Members of the William Strickland family were successful farmers and landowners, and their consumption-related items were undoubtedly used to denote their success. The noticeable archaeological visibility of consumer items at the site also erodes the popular perception of frontier farms as isolated and backward.

Items recovered from the Strickland farm aptly illustrate that consumerism started in the domain of foodways, especially objects associated with entertaining and social contexts. A subsequent trend that develops, as later case studies illustrate, is that non-food-related items, such as personal possessions and household furnishings, become much more prevalent in the archaeological record during the 1800s. Consequently, rural sites from the colonial period can reveal how consumerism began in the domain of food-ways for typical farming households. Later farm sites reveal how consumerism eventually expanded into the areas of personal possessions and household furnishings—those areas that are incredibly underrepresented at most colonial rural sites.

Colonial Life among Chesapeake Farmers

The earliest farming settlements in the Southeast were established during the sixteenth and seventeenth centuries along the Atlantic coast. Settler communities were first established by the Spanish in Florida and South Carolina during the 1500s, by the British in the Virginia Chesapeake during the early 1600s, followed by the British in the South Carolina Low Country in the late 1600s. Farming in this region during the beginning of the colonial period was modest compared to developments between the late colonial and antebellum periods. Typical of multiethnic societies, colonial life along the Atlantic coast was an interesting amalgam of European, West African, and Native American cultural elements. Material culture in the early settlements was late medieval in character accompanied by a thin veneer of formative consumerism. Domestic architecture among farmers, planters, tenants, and slaves alike usually consisted of small, timber-framed structures, typically of earthfast construction (e.g., Kelso 1984; Carson et al. 1988). Differences in social class and affluence among farming households were often denoted by visible differences in the built environment, such as house lot and dwelling size. Conversely, distinctions in social rank between different households, as indicated by archaeologically recovered material culture, were often subtle. In general, the material culture used by farmers and planters from this period often contained better quality ceramics, such as porcelain, larger amounts of flatware, a greater number of artifact categories, and better cuts of meat compared to tenant or slave artifact assemblages.

Jamestown, the first permanent English settlement in North America, was established in 1607 along the James River in Virginia. Over the course of the seventeenth and eighteenth centuries, settlement in Virginia expanded initially from the Chesapeake Bay area into the Virginia Piedmont and Shenandoah Valley. During the first two decades of the colony's history, daily life among Virginia settlers focused upon basic survival. By the early 1620s and through the 1680s, however, the introduction of tobacco created a boom economy in the colony. As Kulikoff (1986) emphasizes, the "Tobacco Coast" of Virginia during this formative colonial period was inhabited by small-scale farmers and planters who worked several hundred acres with their own labor and the assistance of English indentured servants. Tobacco production accelerated in the region during this interval, from 65,000 pounds annually in the 1620s to 20,000,000 pounds annually by the 1670s.

The 1680s were important years of transition in the Chesapeake. The tobacco boom fostered economic and social mobility among many English indentured servants. After satisfying their indenture to a planter, many servants were able to start successful agricultural ventures of their own. The prosperity of the seventeenth-century boom cycle coupled with declining European migration later in the century inadvertently created a labor shortage among tobacco planters. To alleviate these shortages, Virginia tobacco planters began using West African slaves to work their plantations. The boom economy lasted until the early 1700s in Virginia, then was followed by a 50-year depression. By the 1750s, the tobacco economy entered a second upswing or boom cycle that continued through the American Revolution (Kulikoff 1986).

During the colonial period, several different types of tobacco plantations existed in the Virginia Chesapeake, consisting of small, medium, and large plantations. The development of these plantations in turn reflected the history of the larger agricultural system in the Chesapeake region, and generally corresponded to the early, middle, and late colonial periods (Kulikoff 1986). The small-scale tobacco plantation, basically a family-operated farm, was the earliest type of plantation in Virginia. On small plantations, the planter, his wife, their adult children, one or two indentured servants, perhaps a hired hand or, later in time, a few slaves worked several hundred acres of tobacco and also raised subsistence crops (Kulikoff 1986). This rural economic form persisted throughout the colonial and antebellum periods. The planter's household, indentured servants, and later slaves often initially lived in the same dwelling or domestic compound on small plantations during the early colonial period in Virginia before the slavery system fully matured.

The medium-size plantation, the second type of Virginia tobacco plantation, first appeared during the middle colonial period between approximately 1660 and 1750. This period corresponds to the first substantial importation of enslaved West Africans into Virginia. As Kulikoff (1986: 330) states, by the 1730s, "half of the slaves" in the Chesapeake "lived on quarters of ten or fewer, and only a quarter resided on units of more than twenty" slaves. Most medium-sized plantations, not unlike small-scale plantations and farms, probably consisted of relatively small, nucleated domestic complexes containing the main dwelling, outbuildings, and several slave quarters.

The third type of tobacco plantation in the Chesapeake became more prevalent between the 1750s and the close of the colonial period in the 1790s. During this period, the importation of slaves declined and the American-born or native-born slave population increased. As Kulikoff notes (1986: 337), between the 1740s and 1780s, "44 percent of tidewater's blacks lived on farms of more than twenty slaves, and another 26 percent lived on medium-sized units of eleven to twenty. The number of very large quarters also grew. Before the 1740s few quarters housed more than thirty slaves, but by the 1770s and 1780s the wealthiest gentlemen ran home plantations with more than one hundred slaves and quarters with thirty to fifty." The cultural landscape at many large-scale tobacco plantations would probably have contained a dispersed, as opposed to nucleated, settlement pattern, characterized by a main house complex with several outbuildings and one or more separate slave communities or quarters located a discreet distance from the planter's residence.

As discussed above, small-scale farms and plantations in the Chesapeake contained a nucleated lot consisting of a small frame dwelling, outbuildings, adjacent servants' quarters, and fences. Several pertinent archaeological studies illustrate the types of Chesapeake farming communities that existed during the colonial period.

Wolstenholme Towne

The excavations at Wolstenholme Towne (Nöel Hume 1982) aptly illustrate the site structure and architecture typical of early colonial settlements. Similar landscape and architectural elements occur at early colonial farmsteads and plantations throughout the coastal South. Wolstenholme Towne was the fortified administrative center of a larger farming community called Martin's Hundred. Encompassing a 21,500-acre land tract located along the shore of the James River approximately 9 miles below Jamestown, Martin's Hundred was inhabited by 220 English settlers (Figure 1.2). The community was initially supported by private investors beginning in 1618.

Unfortunately, Wolstenholme Towne was one of the hardest hit settlements during the Powhatan Indian revolt, later dubbed the Massacre of 1622

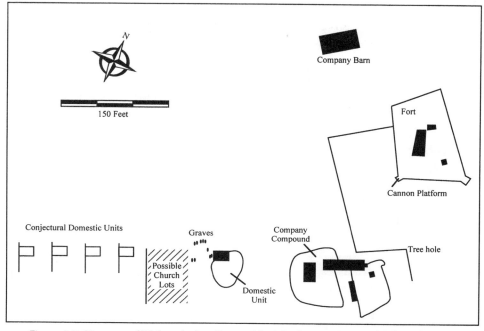

Figure 3.5. Site map of Wolstenholme Towne, Virginia. By permission of Colonial Williamsburg Foundation.

by historians. The surviving settlers rebuilt the settlement but eventually abandoned the community during the latter half of the 1640s. While conducting excavations at the eighteenth-century plantation of Carter's Grove, the original home of Robert "King" Carter, Noël Hume and his colleagues accidentally discovered the remains of Wolstenholme Towne and outlying residences in 1970. Located near Williamsburg, the seventeenth-century settlement was eventually excavated during the late 1970s.

As illustrated in Figure 3.5, Wolstenholme Towne contained a palisaded fort, a company compound, a fenced domestic compound, and a barn in the east half of the site. The western portion of the site, probably containing additional dwellings and perhaps a church, eroded into the James River over the centuries. The settlement plan of Martin's Hundred is thought to have been based upon contemporary seventeenth-century Ulster-Scot settler communities called bawnes. Bawnes were frontier farming settlements located along the Irish borderlands of Britain. Ulster-Scot bawnes contained a row or avenue of residential lots occupied by settler households. The residence of the community leader, located adjacent to the settler lots, was often fortified with a palisade and served as a refuge for the community during times of conflict or danger.

Wolstenholme Towne is archaeologically compelling because it aptly illustrates the built environment and folk-based character of material life that prevailed during the colonial period in the South. These folk traditions, ultimately medieval in origin, are expressed in the site structure, architecture, and household goods encountered at Wolstenholme Towne. Its general site structure is asymmetrical yet nucleated. Paralleling Irish bawnes or farming settlements along the border of Britain and Ireland, the main administrative center contained a cluster of buildings arranged around a skewed quadrangle. Further, earthfast architecture predominated at the site, along with livestock fences of wattle construction that abutted the corners of the post-in-the-ground dwellings. Earthfast architecture (Carson et al. 1988), still used to construct outbuildings in the rural South today, consists of timber-framed structures, both dwellings and outbuildings, with the main wall timbers seated in large postholes. In addition to asymmetrical site structure, earthfast architecture, and wattle fences, the site residents also used locally made lead-glazed ceramics and imported wares.

Within the southern British colonies, the important material elements of asymmetrical or strewn site structure, earthfast architecture, and reliance on both locally manufactured and imported ceramics were first introduced by early seventeenth-century colonists in the Chesapeake and South Carolina. These late medieval cultural elements likewise persisted at many farmsteads and plantations in Virginia and the Carolinas throughout the eighteenth and early nineteenth centuries among all wealth groups. Material culture, especially in the domain of household goods, was modified over time, however, by the addition of non-European elements and contributions from early consumer culture. As the importation of slaves commenced at coastal plantations during the second half of the seventeenth century in Virginia and South Carolina, colono ware (Ferguson 1992) became more prevalent in the archaeological record. Colono ware was used not only by slave households but also by European settlers, as indicated by its recovery from the dwellings of planters and slave-owning farmers. As cultural exchange was occurring between early settler households, a thin veneer of formative consumerism, illustrated by the prevalence of industrially manufactured ceramics at eighteenth-century sites, was eventually added to the folk-based material tradition that was transplanted to the Chesapeake in the seventeenth century.

Kingsmill

Kingsmill was a large tract of land located near Jamestown, Wolstenholme Towne, and Williamsburg along the James River. William Kelso (1984) conducted extensive archaeological investigations at 15 different sites on the Kingsmill tract in response to residential and commercial development in the 1970s. Contemporaneous with Martin's Hundred and Wolstenholme Towne, Kingsmill began as several small tracts that were held by different absentee landowners. Tenant farmers, beginning in the 1620s, initially settled the tracts. The Bray and Burwell families later consolidated the smaller, original parcels into Littletown and Kingsmill plantations, respectively, during the eighteenth century. The archaeology of Kingsmill is significant because it illustrates general material trends associated with small and middling planters, tenant farmers, and slaves during the seventeenth and eighteenth centuries in the Chesapeake and the British colonial South.

Tenant farmers at the Littletown and Kingsmill tenements settled the first tracts between the 1620s and 1650s (Figure 3.6). The domestic complex at the Kingsmill Tenement exhibited a strewn settlement plan, and both

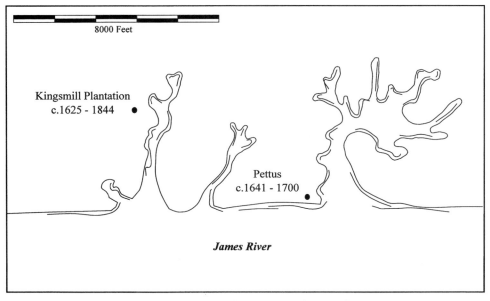

Figure 3.6. Map of Kingsmill Plantation, showing sites discussed in text. By permission of William Kelso.

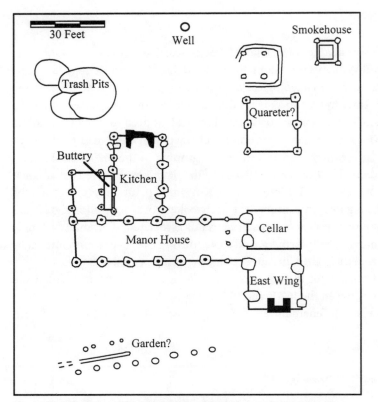

Figure 3.7. Plan view of seventeenth-century house lot at Pettus's Littletown. By permission of William Kelso.

the Kingsmill and Littletown tenements contained large rectangular earthfast dwellings. The principal dwellings at the two tenements were similar in size, measuring approximately 40 by 18 feet and containing four 10-foot bays. The tenements did not contain any brick architectural remains. The dwellings probably had wood and clay chimneys. A few decades after the Littletown and Kingsmill tenements were settled, Thomas Pettus, a landowner, established a residence at nearby Littletown plantation in the 1640s. This plantation remained in the Pettus family until 1710. During the Pettus ownership of Littletown, tenant farmers and slaves produced tobacco at the plantation. During the seventeenth century, the plantation contained a small quadrangular main complex. All of the structures in the complex— the main dwelling, a possible detached quarter, and a smokehouse—were of earthfast construction. Somewhat Z-shaped in appearance, the Pettus main dwelling was a large sprawling earthfast house that was probably enlarged through time as the household required more living space. Forming a long rectangular core, the main dwelling contained three bays measuring 29 by 18 feet. Half-bay wing additions were located near the gable ends of the main core (Figure 3.7). The Pettus dwelling contained two brick chimney bases, a brick-lined cellar, and glass casement windows.

The Utopia tract was a smaller domestic complex owned by the Pettus family. The complex was located east across a drainage from the main Littletown plantation complex. Inhabited by tenants, servants, or slaves, the Utopia dwelling, measuring 29 by 18 feet, was of earthfast construction and contained a brick-lined cellar. Brick hearths were not encountered, suggesting the dwelling contained wood and clay chimneys.

The land encompassing Littletown plantation, previously held by the Pettus family, was later acquired in 1700 by the Bray family through marriage. At this time, James Bray II constructed a wooden frame dwelling with a brick foundation and a full basement measuring 29 x 53 feet. Feature fill and ceramics from the cellar indicate the structure burned in about 1780. In contrast to the extensive use of earthfast construction among all social segments in the seventeenth century, during the early eighteenth century planters at Kingsmill, like Bray and Burwell, began using brick architecture as a form of social differentiation. Earthfast architecture continued to be used in the region but was more prevalent among middle and lower social classes, represented by middle-sized and small-scale planters, farmers, and slaves.

Social distance between planters and laborers was also reinforced at Littletown during this period by a dispersed settlement pattern. Enslaved laborers resided at the Tuttey's Neck and Utopia sections of the plantation, areas that were a significant distance from the main residential complex. During its operation by the Bray family, Littletown was a large-scale plantation, with approximately 80 slaves between the 1720s and 1740s. During this period, a diversified production strategy was implemented at the plantation, and enslaved laborers raised tobacco, corn, wheat, and livestock. The plantation also contained a gristmill, leather tannery, brickworks, and sawmill. Littletown plantation remained in the Bray family until the Burwell family acquired it, and it became part of Kingsmill plantation in 1796.

As Littletown plantation was maturing into a large-scale agricultural venture, Lewis Burwell III inherited a large segment of land adjacent to Littletown in 1719 and named the tract Kingsmill. Containing a Palladian-influenced brick mansion and a formally landscaped domestic compound and garden, by 1735 the main complex at Kingsmill was a showplace estate

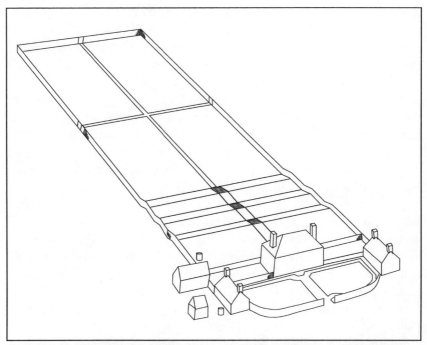

Figure 3.8. Map showing landscape design used at Burwell's Kingsmill Plantation. By permission of William Kelso.

along the James River (Figure 3.8). The brick mansion at Burwell's Kingsmill contained a four-course thick brick foundation in English bond measuring 61 by 40 feet. The manor house was a two-story dwelling with four rooms on each floor. The central complex also contained symmetrically placed flanking buildings that were situated at right angles in the front of the brick dwelling facing the main road. A terraced lawn and a large rectangular garden were located in the rear yard of the complex overlooking the James River. Approximately 50 years later, Lewis Burwell V sold Kingsmill plantation. The brick mansion was destroyed by fire in 1844, but the residential complex continued to be used by later owners until the early twentieth century.

In summary, the area encompassing Colonial Williamsburg, Wolstenholme Towne, and Kingsmill illustrates the development of early farming cultures during the colonial period in the South. During the 1600s, material life in coastal colonial settlements was vernacular based, drawing influence from the late medieval period that was coming to a close in rural areas of Western Europe. Late medieval culture from Europe in turn intersected with Native American and African cultures in the Tidewater South, eventually forging a distinctive regional tradition during the ensuing 1700s and 1800s.

Much of the population in the Tidewater during the early colonial period resided in dwellings of timber-frame construction with the main wall supports seated in substantial postholes. These typically small structures were covered with clapboards and heated with wood and clay chimneys. The households' furnishings were sparse—sleeping mats or ticks (often placed directly on the ground), a chest for clothes and other personal items, and a table and chairs or benches. The residents used coarse utilitarian ceramics, both imported and locally made, and relied upon livestock and crops for most of their dietary needs.

During the latter half of the colonial period, frame dwellings of successful farmers and planters became more substantial with continuous brick foundations or brick pier supports. The furnishings also became more comfortable as the amount of commercial goods used by southern rural households increased. The house lots at these later colonial farms also became more organized, with outbuildings arranged in planned landscape patterns rather than being haphazardly placed in the farm lot. Among slaves and tenants on small farms and plantations, living conditions that first appeared during the colonial period persisted throughout the remainder of the colonial and antebellum periods.

French Colonial Farms in the Illinois Country

The American Midwest was a territory of New France during the colonial period. Initially established in 1534 when Cartier explored the St. Lawrence River valley, at its peak in the early 1700s the territory of New France encompassed a large swath of North America. In the early 1700s New France extended from the Gulf coast area of Louisiana and Alabama, north through the Mississippi Valley to the Great Lakes, and east to the St. Lawrence River valley, through New England, and farther north to Labrador and Hudson Bay in Canada. New France had five colonies—Louisiana, Canada, Acadia, Newfoundland, and Hudson Bay. By 1763 much of this area was ceded to the British at the close of the French and Indian War. In 1803, Napoleon retook the Louisiana territory held by Spain since the end of the French and Indian War and subsequently sold this vast tract to the United States as the Louisiana Purchase (Walthall and Emerson 1991: 4–11; Brown and Dean 1995: 1–2).

The colonial Midwest was called the Illinois Country and was a part of the Louisiana Colony. The Illinois Country, encompassing parts of modern-day Illinois, Indiana, Missouri, and Ohio, was also known as Upper Louisiana. The region, named after the Illinois Indians who inhabited the region during the early historic period, was initially called the Western Country. French explorer Jean Nicollet landed at Green Bay in 1634, followed by the expeditions of Jolliet and Marquette in 1673 and La Salle in 1679. Louis Jolliet and Father Jacques Marquette were two of the first Europeans to travel extensively in the Western Country, exploring Lake Michigan and the Mississippi and Illinois rivers in 1673. Later, in 1679, La Salle traversed the Illinois Country and reached the mouth of the Mississippi River. For approximately 75 years after these early expeditions, missions, trading posts, forts, and settler communities were established along the middle Mississippi River valley, the core area of the French Illinois Country, in locations such as Cahokia, Kaskaskia, Prairie du Rocher, Ste. Genevieve, and St. Louis (Walthall and Emerson 1991: 4–11; Brown and Dean 1995: 1–2).

Archaeologists divide the colonial era in the Illinois Country into three main culture history periods: the exploration period (1634–1717), the colonization period (1717–1765), and the Creole period (1765–1803) (Walthall and Emerson 1991: 3–13). From the 1670s to the 1710s in the Illinois Country, the frontier economy focused primarily upon the Indian trade between Native Americans and French Indian traders called the voyageurs. The voyageurs traveled by flat-bottomed riverboats called *bateaux* and canoes called *pirogues* throughout the Illinois Country and traded with Native Americans, exchanging animal skins supplied by the Indians for trade goods manufactured in Europe, such as firearms, knives and hatchets, metal cooking utensils, cloth, and personal items such as beads, mirrors, and jewelry (Walthall and Emerson 1991: 4–11; Brown and Dean 1995: 1–10). The Indian trade was a major source of culture change among Native Americans in North America.

From the late 1710s to the early 1800s, economic activities centered increasingly upon agriculture conducted by farming households in settler communities located across the Illinois Country. The French government particularly encouraged the development of agricultural communities in the Illinois Country so settlers would be economically independent and self-sufficient. French colonial farmers practiced small-scale grain and livestock agriculture. French settlers raised corn, wheat, and rye, and milled flour became an important agricultural trade item produced in the Illinois Country. The raising of livestock, especially pork and cattle, was also an important farm activity (Brown and Dean 1995: 5–6).

During the 1700s, French settlers and farm families, called *habitants*, relied upon several distinctive cultural practices in the New World. In turn, these cultural practices have material implications that are significant for historical archaeologists conducting excavations at sites occupied by the French during the colonial period. These practices are particularly evident in the material domains of settlement patterns, farmstead spatial organization, and domestic architecture.

Regarding settlement patterns, French colonists in the Illinois Country, often having migrated from the Gulf region or Canada, established residences along major rivers to encourage efficient transportation of people and goods. The French settlers were granted distinctive plots of land, typically rectangular in shape, by the colonial government. French colonial farmsteads were usually only one or two arpents wide and about 50 arpents in length. (The arpent was a French unit of land measurement that corresponded to approximately 192 linear feet.) Within these long, narrow, rectangular farmsteads, the main complex containing the farmhouse and outbuildings was located adjacent to the river, and the farm's fields were located in the rear of the rectangular lot (Figure 3.9) (Brown and Dean 1995: 9).

Archaeological and documentary research conducted at Old Town Ste. Genevieve in Missouri illustrates the settlement patterns associated with French farmsteads and villages in the Illinois Country (Figure 1.2). The French village of Old Town Ste. Genevieve, located near the modern community of Ste. Genevieve, Missouri, was established about 1750 on the west bank of the Mississippi River. Research conducted by Norris (1991) indicates that the inhabitants of the community used a dual settlement system. For example, a 1793 map of the town indicates that rectangular farm lots arranged in a linear "string town" configuration were sited adjacent to the Mississippi River, conforming to settlement patterns typically associated with French colonial farmsteads. Conversely, other period maps and archaeologically recorded domestic sites indicate that Old Town Ste. Genevieve also contained a nucleated village center, probably arranged in a grid pattern. This settlement dichotomy initially seems confusing, but as Norris (1991: 145) notes, farming households would have resided in the linear lots fronting the river,

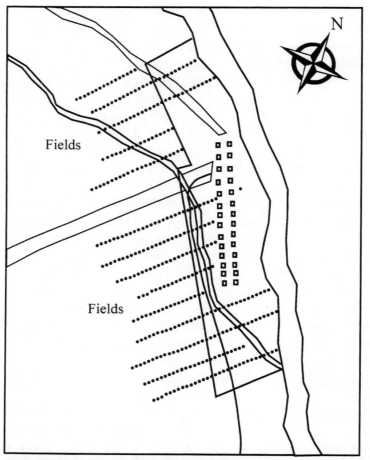

Figure 3.9. Map of French linear farms at Old Town Ste. Genevieve, ca. 1793. From *French Colonial Archaeology: The Illinois Country and the Western Great Lakes*. Copyright 1991 by the Board of Trustees of the University of Illinois. Used with permission of the University of Illinois Press.

and nonfarming households, individuals engaged in skilled trades such as craftspersons and merchants, would have benefited economically by living in the town.

In addition to settlement patterns, the site structure of farmsteads is also an important topic studied by historical archaeologists. Site structure at historic residences refers to the spatial arrangement and internal archaeological contents of the house lot. The location of the dwelling and other lot elements, such as outbuildings, fences, and refuse disposal areas, are typical questions addressed by archaeologists when they reconstruct the site structure of an excavated farm lot. In some situations, the dwelling or a few outbuildings may still be present at a study site. In other situations, such as French colonial sites in the Illinois Country, few aboveground architectural features would have survived to the present.

The site structure of French farm and village house lots was internally similar. As Brown and Dean (1995: 10) state, French colonial house lots would have typically been rectangular or square in shape, fenced with post and pale or picket fences, and containing the dwelling, a vegetable garden, a small orchard, a well, possibly a privy, a pigeon house, hen house, and a stable (Figure 3.10). French colonial farmers constructed large barns, measuring about 60 by 60 feet, which were located near the house lot or near the fields. French settlers also used distinctive outdoor domed bread ovens. These ovens were often 6 by 3 feet in size and constructed of a wooden frame covered with puddled clay that was fired to a brick-like hardness.

Although generally similar to dwellings built by colonial frontier settlers along the Atlantic rim, French dwellings possessed several distinctive architectural elements that distinguish them from the houses of British or Spanish settlers. French colonial dwellings were generally built of wood, stone, or brick. With origins in the medieval period of Europe, wooden French colonial dwellings were examples of impermanent domestic architecture (Carson et al. 1988), meaning they were not built to last for long periods of time but were frontier residences expected to have a use-life of 10 to 20 years.

Wooden timber frame structures in which the vertical upright wall posts were anchored in the ground was a prevalent type of French impermanent architecture. Called *poteaux en terre* (meaning posts in the earth), the wall posts of these houses were seated in large postholes (Gums et al. 1991: 91–92; Brown and Dean 1995: 9). French post-in-the-ground structures also often contained wall trenches. A narrow trench was dug that formed the outline of the structure, and wall timbers were seated in postholes excavated into the trench at specific intervals. Also called earthfast construction, the use of post-in-the ground dwellings was widespread among the French and other New World settlers during the colonial period. However, the use of wall trenches was found mainly among the French, Native Americans, and enslaved Africans during the early colonial period in eastern North America. As might be expected, however, the wall posts placed in the ground were susceptible to rotting from moisture and damage from insects, which limited their lifespan and required periodic maintenance and repair.

Poteaux sur sole (meaning posts on sill) was another type of imperma-

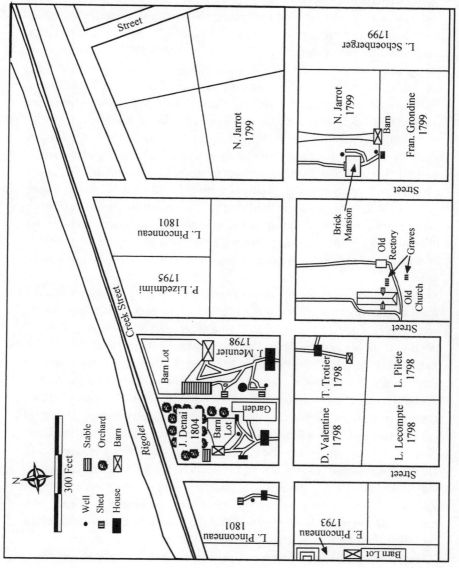

Figure 3.10. Examples of colonial French house lots at Cahokia, ca. 1790–1826. From *French Colonial Archaeology: The Illinois Country and the Western Great Lakes.* Copyright 1991 by the Board of Trustees of the University of Illinois. Used with permission of the University of Illinois Press.

nent architecture used by the French in the Illinois Country. With this construction, the wooden foundation sills of a structure were placed directly on the ground (Gums et al. 1991: 91–92; Brown and Dean 1995: 9). Wall timbers were then seated on top of the horizontally placed wooden sill to construct the frame. Wooden *poteaux sur sole* foundation sills were also susceptible to decay from the elements, since the wood was in direct contact with the ground surface. In some situations, the wooden wall sills were placed on top of an actual stone foundation, which was a more durable and permanent type of construction method.

French wooden frame dwellings usually contained wall timbers or framing studs spaced at equal intervals approximately 2 to 3 feet apart. The space between the framing timbers was filled with several different types of material. Some timber dwellings had walls filled with *bousillage*, a mixture of clay and straw (Brown and Dean 1995: 9). Wattle and daub was another method of filling walls of frame houses. A wicker-work lattice or lathe called wattle was constructed from branches woven between the wall timbers. The wattle fabric was then plastered with clay (called daub). Upon drying, the daub plaster achieved a brick-like hardness. Brick filling in the walls of timber frame structures was also another method of wall construction. This method was less prevalent because of the cost of making bricks during the colonial period. With brick-filled walls, brick courses were placed between the vertical wall posts. Only a few examples of colonial earthfast structures with brick-filled walls have been archaeologically documented in eastern North America (e.g., Forehand et al. 2004). In addition to post-in-the-ground and post-on-sill architecture, the colonial French also constructed log houses. The use of horizontally placed hewn timbers to construct the walls of dwellings was called *piece sur piece* by the French (Brown and Dean 1995: 9).

Stone construction, although rare, was used by the French in the Illinois Country, usually by wealthy individuals who could afford the high cost of stone masonry. Stone construction, though less prevalent in domestic residences, was used by the colonial French for some public buildings, such as churches and courthouses (Brown and Dean 1995: 9).

The dwellings of French settlers and farmers in the Illinois Country were usually small, measuring about 16 by 25 feet. They were a story-and-a-half in height with two main rooms on the ground floor and steeply pitched roofs covered with thatch or wooden shingles. The lofts in the attics were used for storage or as extra sleeping quarters. French colonial houses also had one or two fireplaces, constructed of stone, brick, or, more commonly, wood and clay, in which a wooden frame was covered with clay daub. French dwell-

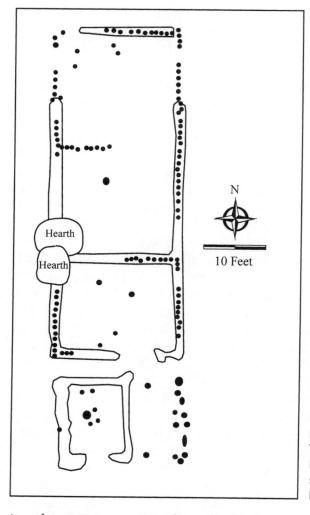

Figure 3.11. Plan view of colonial French barracks excavated at Fort Massac in southern Illinois. From *French Colonial Archaeology: The Illinois Country and the Western Great Lakes.* Copyright 1991 by the Board of Trustees of the University of Illinois. Used with permission of the University of Illinois Press.

ings also sometimes contained a small cellar for storage. To create additional domestic space during the warm months, French houses also had a porch or *galerie* on two or all four sides of the structure (Brown and Dean 1995: 9–10). The architectural elements of timber frame construction, a steeply pitched roof, and a wraparound porch gave French colonial farm houses a distinctive appearance.

Although few French colonial farmhouses have been examined archaeologically, several examples of dwellings and public buildings have been investigated archaeologically in the Illinois Country. These previously investigated structures provide important comparative information regarding the architecture present at French farmsteads. At Fort Massac near Metropolis in southern Illinois, archaeologists hired by the Works Progress Administration (WPA) excavated the entire French and Indian War period fort and encountered two large barracks of *poteaux en terre* construction. The barracks measured about 60 by 18 feet. The walls of the structures had been built by excavating narrow wall trenches and placing wall posts at intervals in the wall trenches (Figure 3.11). The walls were then filled with mortar. The presence of ash-filled pits and large rocks indicate that the structures contained hearths (Walthall 1991: 52–55). Similar types of architecture were probably used at French farms.

At Cahokia in East St. Louis, Missouri, the foundation of the Cahokia Courthouse was excavated by archaeologists hired by the WPA during reconstruction of the structure. The structure is thought to have been built in the early 1740s and initially served as a dwelling until 1793, when it was purchased by St. Clair County; it served as a courthouse until 1814 when the county seat was moved to Belleville. During the remainder of the nineteenth century it was used as a residence for a short interval and then served as a town hall, warehouse, and saloon. Based on the results of archaeological excavation, it was eventually reconstructed in 1940 through support from the WPA (Gums et al. 1991: 92–99).

The excavations conducted in 1938 revealed that a combination of post-on-sill and post-in-the-ground construction techniques had been used to build the structure. Its main core had rested on a limestone foundation (Figure 3.12). The walls of the main structure were constructed of vertical timbers seated on a wooden sill that rested on the limestone foundation. The east and west sides of the structure also contained lean-to additions, indicated by wall trenches of post-in-the-ground construction encountered in these areas during the WPA excavations. The additions were 16 feet wide and at least 25 feet in length, although the full length was not determined by the excavations (Gums et al. 1991: 92–91).

Excavations conducted in 1986 by archaeologists with the University of Missouri, Columbia, also revealed important information about French domestic architecture in the Illinois Country. This type of architecture was likewise undoubtedly used by French farm families during the colonial period. Field investigations were conducted near Ste. Genevieve, south of St. Louis, along the Saline Creek valley, a major location of colonial salt production owing to the presence of natural salt springs in the area. Fieldwork conducted near the salt spring and salt furnace complex in an area designated Concentration C revealed the presence of an early *poteaux en*

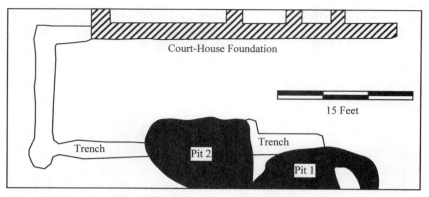

Figure 3.12. Plan view of the colonial French Cahokia Courthouse in East St. Louis, Missouri. From *French Colonial Archaeology: The Illinois Country and the Western Great Lakes*. Copyright 1991 by the Board of Trustees of the University of Illinois. Used with permission of the University of Illinois Press.

terre structure (Figure 3.13). Defined by a wall trench, the structure was about 15 by 12 feet and contained a chimney in the southwest corner of the dwelling. A pit cellar measuring about 9 by 9 by 1.5 feet was also located along the south wall near the chimney (Trimble et al. 1991: 180–181). Ceramics obtained from surface collection prior to excavations indicate that the dwelling was occupied between ca. 1750 and 1820.

Artifacts recovered from the dwelling—a cowbell, cauldron base, ceramics, brass buttons, gun parts, hundreds of faunal remains, and ceramics—illustrate the domestic function of the structure. Creamware ceramics, pearlware (underglaze blue handpainted, transfer-printed, and edge-decorated wares), Chinese export porcelain, Jackfield, and faience were recovered. Further, although the residents of the structure were probably involved in salt production at Saline Creek, the faunal assemblage illustrates that agriculture and animal husbandry were part of daily life at the settlement. Pig remains were the predominant food resource in the assemblage, and the pig and cow remains exhibited butchering marks. Horse, goat, deer, wild turkey, and mallard duck were also identified in the faunal assemblage (Trimble et al. 1991: 181–184).

In addition to material characteristics associated with settlement patterns, farmstead spatial organization, and domestic architecture, historical archaeologists have also studied the types of household goods and foodstuffs that French colonial settlers and farm households relied upon in the Illinois Country. As illustrated by the dwelling in Concentration C along the Saline Creek, the artifact assemblages from most colonial domestic sites

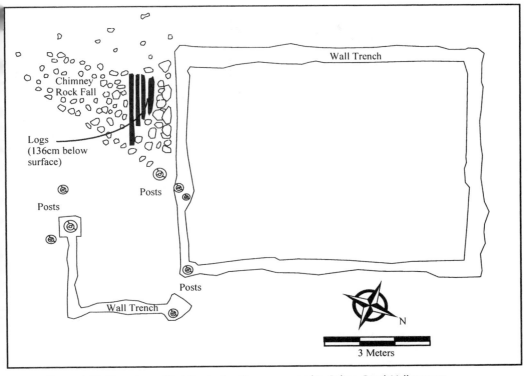

Figure 3.13. Plan view of *habitants* dwelling excavated in Saline Creek Valley near Ste. Genevieve, Missouri. From *French Colonial Archaeology: The Illinois Country and the Western Great Lakes.* Copyright 1991 by the Board of Trustees of the University of Illinois. Used with permission of the University of Illinois Press.

usually contain a predominance of kitchen and architectural-related artifacts. Conversely, artifacts not related to kitchen activities or architecture, such as beads, coins, or fragments of children's toys, are not often abundant at colonial frontier sites. As discussed in subsequent chapters, the noticeable increase in material consumption and discard is a major trend at domestic sites occupied during the postcolonial period.

At colonial French sites, kitchen and food-related artifacts generally consist of ceramics and glassware and the animal bones, called faunal remains, from meals. French colonial domestic sites often contain French ceramics called faience, a type of ceramic tableware that has a tin glaze. French faience was produced in a range of vessel forms such as plates and platters. In addition to faience, lead-glazed coarse earthenwares used for food preparation, storage, and consumption are typical ceramics found at French colonial sites. Likewise, because of factors related to market access in frontier contexts and the expansion of industrially manufactured pottery after the 1750s, French residences and farmsteads also often contain British manufactured wares, such as white saltglaze, creamware, and pearlware table vessels (Walthall 1991: 55–64).

During the twentieth century, historical archaeologists assembled a considerable amount of information about French colonial life in the Illinois Country. However, as John Walthall (1991: 11–13) emphasizes in the introduction to *French Colonial Archaeology*, there is still a large amount of archaeological work to be conducted and a broad range of research questions that remain to be addressed concerning this topic. Walthall notes that there are large artifact collections from earlier fort excavations that could be the subject of collections research, such as the material from Fort Massac and Fort de Chartres. Likewise, he stresses that detailed investigations of French villages and farmsteads have been neglected, and "Archaeological evidence of the life of the French *habitants* is virtually unknown" (Walthall 1991: 12). Further, the cultural transformation that occurred during the transition from the French colonial period to the early American period in the region after the Louisiana Purchase in 1803 has not been intensively addressed. Considered together, these observations concerning the current state of knowledge for French colonial archaeology in the Midwest should not be viewed as shortcomings of previous researchers; rather, they illustrate exciting new paths of inquiry for future historical archaeologists.

Conclusion

The preceding case studies illustrate that colonial farmsteads are fascinating and important archaeological resources. These farmsteads reveal the material conditions that prevailed at the beginning of settlement in North America and also show how colonial frontier conditions stabilized and diminished over time as the colonial period drew to a close. Consequently, these archaeological resources illustrate the beginning of rural life in the United States and also illustrate material conditions on the eve of the nation's birth.

Colonial farmsteads within the three regions considered in this chapter— the Northeast, the Southeast, and the Midwest—shared several cultural and archaeological characteristics. During the colonial period, eastern North America was a peripheral or marginal area within the expanding world economy. After farms were settled in frontier regions, colonial households engaged in varying levels of commercial agriculture, striving to raise agricultural products for local, regional, and national markets. Consequently, economic activities connected frontier farming households to the world beyond their communities. These rural economic activities in turn were a catalyst for eventual material change among farm families.

Colonial settlers in eastern North America depended upon vernacular knowledge to create their domestic landscapes. Revealing late medieval material influences, most colonial farm lots were arranged asymmetrically and grew over time according to household need. Colonists likewise depended upon impermanent domestic architecture, such as the use of earthfast dwellings or log construction, to a great extent. Although the domestic landscape at many colonial farmsteads was rough-hewn and unrefined, archaeology reveals that within colonial farmhouses, settlers were aware of popular fashion trends. Betraying the stereotype of the colonial frontier as a geographically isolated place, the recovery of industrially and locally manufactured ceramics, tobacco pipes, glass bottle fragments, and personal items, such as pocket knives, straight razors, and keys, subtly illustrates the thin veneer of formative consumerism that colonial farmers participated in.

If early colonial farmsteads illustrate the beginning of rural material life in eastern North America, then later colonial sites show how frontier conditions stabilized and diminished at the end of the 1700s. Later colonial farms also illustrate the beginning of material trends that would come to dominate the 1800s. Spatial organization within many colonial farmhouse lots became structured, standardized, organized, and often symmetrical or balanced. Dwellings were also increasingly built of brick or wood with brick foundations to last longer than the lives of their owners. Within archaeologically excavated deposits, such as sheet midden created outside of rear doors and within refuse pits, the amount of manufactured items used and discarded at late colonial farmsteads also begins to increase perceptibly as colonial transportation and marketing systems mature. Many of these material trends within the domestic landscape and household at farmsteads, in turn, become even more pronounced during the ensuing antebellum period.

4

Federal and Antebellum Farmsteads

Between the early 1800s and the 1860s, several important trends influenced daily life among rural households. During the first half of the nineteenth century, communities along the eastern seaboard matured from colonial footholds to established towns and cities. Many of these early cities, such as Boston, New York, Philadelphia, Baltimore, Richmond, Charleston, and Savannah, became important regional economic centers. They also developed into market locations for the redistribution of farm products and manufactured goods. Meanwhile, the American frontier continued to expand west across the Appalachian-Allegheny Mountains until settlement extended beyond the Mississippi River. During this period, frontier conditions persisted in many parts of the Middle South, the Gulf coastal states, and the Midwest. Paralleling characteristics of the colonial frontier, settlers during the early to middle 1800s were often members of vernacular or folk-based ethnic cultures and relied upon preindustrial technology and household items. They typically resided in rustic log or frame houses, made many of the items needed for daily life, such as furniture and clothes, and mainly practiced subsistence-level agriculture, at least during the initial years of settling a new home place. Shortly after establishing a satisfactory domicile on the American frontier, however, many rural households began to participate in commercial economies with the intent of making money from the marketing of crops and other farm goods.

As frontier conditions diminished in settled areas, the infrastructure grew along with the rural commercial economy. With the formalization of the farm economy in rural areas, the local and regional infrastructure of settlements became stronger: frontier wagon trails were replaced by well-constructed roads, rivers were cleared and dredged to allow riverboat navigation, canals were created in landlocked areas without access to navigable water, and by the 1830s and 1840s the railroad began a dramatic revolution of the transportation and economic life in many parts of the United States. With the development of transportation systems and formal, cash-based economies, residents of the United States also experienced greater access to the consumer goods being produced in the factories of America and Europe.

These significant, intertwined processes—immigration, settlement expansion, economic growth, infrastructure development, and consumerism—are prominent research themes explored by historical archaeologists excavating farmsteads occupied during the federal and antebellum periods. All of these trends had a substantial influence upon the daily life of farm families during the first half of the nineteenth century. The effects of these far-reaching historical, cultural, and economic processes on farm families were compounded by the profound influence of industrialization, popular culture, and consumerism. Consumerism and popular culture progressed slowly during the eighteenth century but developed into a substantial force of culture change by the mid-nineteenth century, reaching households in cities, towns, and the countryside.

The long-term effect of nineteenth-century industrialization, consumerism, and popular culture can be summarized through a single pervasive concept: standardization. Standardization, an idea originating in industry, refers to the manufacturing process in which identical items are mass produced and assembled on factory lines. It is a taken-for-granted concept that saturates our daily material existence in the twenty-first century, one which began in the mid-eighteenth century and spread through the nineteenth century. Although typically associated with factory-produced goods, much of American material life likewise became standardized during the 1800s, resulting in slow but persistent homogenization of material culture. Differences certainly continued to persist among different cultural, ethnic, linguistic, racial, and socioeconomic groups and between different regions, yet nationally, household material culture began to become standardized. Moreover, although different households participated differently in consumerism, most households, regardless of ethnicity, socioeconomic class, and race, began using greater amounts of consumer items during this period. This material homogenization process, originating with the growth of a formal, commercial economy, resulted in an eventual "sameness" that permeated much of household material life.

For example, many farmers in the 1800s became influenced by ideas of efficiency, labor-saving technology, and profit maximization. These concepts originated with industry and spread into progressive farming through agricultural journals and newspapers. As noted in an important study by Sally McMurry (1988), the farm lot, including the arrangement and function of outbuildings, and the farmhouse, encompassing architectural styles, floor plans, and room function, became increasingly organized and planned or standardized as concepts related to progressive farming became more prevalent. Once characterized by strewn farm lots in which outbuildings and farmhouses were haphazardly scattered across the domestic landscape, a greater number of farmsteads began to be built in neat rectangular or square compounds organized according to principles of efficiency, building function, and planned landscape design. The end result of this standardization process is that many farms dating from the second quarter of the 1800s to the middle 1900s, although not identical, appear similar in the arrangement of the farm lot and the styles of farm dwellings.

Standardization was not limited to the spatial arrangement of farm lots and dwelling styles but was also evident in household furnishings and consumer products purchased at local stores by rural households. Factory-produced furnishings, such as kerosene lamps, mantle clocks, ceramic tableware, and cutlery, became increasingly prevalent. Product name brands and product loyalty, widespread in our own time, also increasingly appeared during the 1800s in the United States, especially after the 1820s, as illustrated by newspaper advertisements from the period. Besides the products themselves, the containers that commercial goods were marketed in became standardized because of the industrialization of the glass industry.

The archaeological effect of the consumer revolution is that farmsteads inhabited during the second half of the nineteenth century, no longer geographically or culturally isolated, often contain an incredibly large amount of discarded industrially manufactured items: ceramic tableware, kitchenware, glassware, window glass, cut nails, metal hardware, clothing items, and personal objects. Mass production and consumption were on the rise, and the prevalence of consumer goods at farmsteads illustrates the spread of this important cultural process into rural contexts during the 1800s.

The challenge for historical archaeologists is to reconstruct the trajectory of important cultural processes, such as settlement expansion, economic growth, infrastructure development, and consumerism, and explore how these trends influenced (or did not influence) daily life at farmsteads occupied between the early 1800s and 1860s. Further, it should also be emphasized that different racial, ethnic, and socioeconomic groups in rural settings may have responded differently to these larger trends that were occurring nationally. Some households may have enthusiastically embraced commercial farming, and others may have resisted becoming enmeshed in extralocal commercial economies. The following case studies illustrate relevant archaeological examples of farmsteads occupied during this dynamic period in America's history.

Historical Archaeology at the Shaeffer Site, a Northern Appalachian Farmstead

Appalachia, extending from the mountains of southern New York to central Alabama, encompasses a substantial 200,000-square-mile area in the eastern United States. Historical archaeology conducted at the Shaeffer site in western Pennsylvania (Figure 1.2) illustrates material characteristics of a nineteenth-century Northern Appalachian farmstead. The Shaeffer farm site, located in Valley Township, Armstrong County, was discovered during the survey of an 80-foot-wide pipeline corridor for a cultural resource management study (Petraglia et al. 1992a, 1992b). The site was later the subject of a data-recovery archaeology project (Bedell et al. 1993). The Shaeffer farm was evaluated as archaeologically significant because, as Bedell and colleagues emphasize (Bedell et al. 1994: 29), "The historical archaeology of western Pennsylvania has been studied little, and important questions about the lives of the residents in the eighteenth and nineteenth centuries have therefore remained unanswered and essentially undiscussed."

The Shaeffer farm was located in the hill country of western Pennsylvania, specifically the Pittsburgh Low Plateau physiographic section of the state. Unlike areas inhabited much earlier in the state, western Pennsylvania was a frontier-like area that remained sparsely settled in 1830 when the George B. Shaeffer family established their farmstead. George Shaeffer later retired in 1848 at the age of sixty-three, and the farm was operated by his son Charles, who resided in a separate dwelling near his parents' residence. Twenty years after settling the farm, George Shaeffer, his wife, Mary, their two sons, and seven daughters were listed in the 1850 population census. George died by 1860, and the farm was operated by his son Charles until 1864. In 1864 the farm was sold by Charles to absentee owners, and his parents' farmhouse was subsequently occupied by tenants until it was abandoned in the early 1900s.

Based on the amount of assets listed in the agricultural censuses, the George Shaeffer family was a member of the rural middle class in Armstrong County. Although the identities of the tenants who resided at the Shaeffer farmhouse after 1864 are not known, on average in the 1860 census for Valley Township, non-landholding males comprised the lowest economic group,

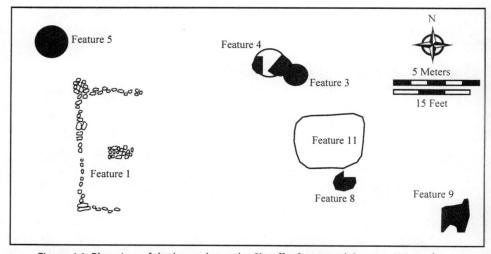

Figure 4.1. Plan view of the house lot at the Shaeffer farmstead. By permission of *Northeast Historical Archaeology*, from Bedell et al. 1994, Figure 3, p. 34.

suggesting tenants at the farm probably experienced a diminished standard of living compared to the Shaeffer family. Consequently, the Shaeffer farm offers the opportunity to explore antebellum material conditions for farm owners and subsequent material characteristics for postbellum farm tenants at a single residence in western Pennsylvania.

During archaeological investigations at the Shaeffer house lot, a 14 percent sample of the site was excavated, consisting of 97 1-by-1-meter excavation squares located in the 80-foot-wide survey corridor of the proposed utility pipeline. Archaeologists conducting cultural resource management studies often use site sampling methods in which a small portion of a site is excavated, with the intent that the excavated area will be representative of the larger archaeological contents of the site. Site sampling, based on statistical concepts, is useful during archaeological projects when it is often not practical or financially feasible to excavate an entire site.

Excavations at the Shaeffer site revealed that the house lot was relatively small, measuring about 70 by 50 feet. The foundation of the original dwelling, the foundation remnants of a small outbuilding, and four pits of unknown function were uncovered during excavations at the farm (Figure 4.1). The outbuilding was located about 30 feet east of the dwelling and was sited on a small horizontal bench measuring approximately 3 by 10 feet that was cut into the side slope of the farm lot. The exact function of the outbuilding was not determined. The four pits were located northwest, northeast, and east of the dwelling. In addition to the archaeological features encountered at the site, 8,780 artifacts were also recovered during excavation, consisting of household items and the animal bones from meals consumed by the farm residents.

Beyond the basic function of providing shelter for a household, farm dwellings are important anthropologically and archaeologically. They can potentially reveal important cultural information about the residents of a site, such as their ethnicity, place of origin, economic priorities, and the life history of the family that resided in a house. The excavated remains of the dwelling at the Shaeffer farm consisted of a partially preserved foundation of uncut, dry-laid stone blocks. Based on the preserved foundation, the farm house at the Shaeffer site measured about 28 feet north-south by 14 feet east-west, comprising 392 square feet. The dwelling was located on a gradual slope near a spring and 130 feet from a small stream.

The dwelling at the Shaeffer farm is thought to have been a log house, based on the foundation encountered archaeologically and known regional trends in the vernacular architecture of western Pennsylvania. The log house, an archetypal form of vernacular architecture in America, was originally constructed throughout many parts of Europe, such as the British Isles and Germany. Old World settlers in turn established this architectural style in the forests of eastern North America between the 1600s and 1800s, and it is one of the most prevalent types of early rural houses in western Pennsylvania, an area populated by German immigrants. Similar to the foundation encountered at the Shaeffer farm, log houses at frontier residences were often built on relatively insubstantial dry-laid stone foundations that did not require mortar.

Paralleling this architectural characteristic associated with the stone foundations of pioneer log houses, little mortar was recovered from the excavations of the house's foundation at the Shaeffer site. The log house at the Shaeffer farm had a central chimney, possibly of wood and clay construction. Wood and clay chimneys on dwellings were prevalent during the frontier period. The house also had several glass windows. It was probably a story-and-a-half in height with a sleeping loft in the attic. The dates of artifacts recovered from the interior of the dwelling in the area beneath the floor suggest that the log house began as a single-room dwelling measuring about 14 by 14 feet square. A second pen of the same size was later added to the log structure, probably during the Shaeffer ownership of the farm, which doubled the length of the house. During the antebellum period large farm families were typical, and the Shaeffer family conformed to this demographic pattern. In 1850 the Shaeffer family consisted of parents George and Mary and nine children of varying ages from infants to young adults in their early twenties. Based on the size of the household between the 1830s and 1860s, the second pen of the log dwelling was probably constructed during this period.

Site excavations at the Shaeffer site revealed the type of dwelling the farm family lived in, and the recovered artifacts illustrate material characteristics of rural life in western Pennsylvania during the 1800s. Perhaps typical of rural material conditions, the majority of artifacts from site excavation were related to architecture and food consumption. Architectural artifacts comprised 43 percent (n=3,780) of the site sample. Foodways and other domestic items, including kitchen artifacts and animal bones, comprised 54 percent (n=4,844) of the artifact total. The remaining 3 percent of the artifacts from the site was thinly distributed among the categories of personal items, arms-related artifacts, and several other miscellaneous artifact categories.

Ceramics and animal bones from meals were the most prevalent artifacts recovered from the excavations conducted in the house lot at the Shaeffer farm. Functional analysis of the recovered ceramics by minimum vessel count, a conservative estimate of ceramic forms based on the grouping of similar vessel sherds, indicate that the ceramics used at the site were evenly distributed between flatwares (n=72), such as plates and saucers, and hollowwares, such as small bowls (n=80) that were used during meals. This information suggests that formal portioned meals were consumed from plates as well as meals from bowls, such as stews. Considered together, dining vessels comprised 40 percent of the total ceramic sample, followed by beverage-related ceramics (35 percent) and food preparation and storage vessels (23 percent). Put another way, three-quarters of the ceramics were used during meals, and a quarter were used for food preparation and storage.

Animal bones from meals are prevalent artifacts at most historic sites. The faunal remains from the farm illustrate that the types of meat consumed by the site residents were relatively consistent throughout its occupation by the Shaeffer family and later tenants. A sample of 561 identified animal bones indicates that pork was the meat of choice among the site residents throughout its occupation, followed by beef and chicken to a much lesser extent. A small amount of wild game was also consumed during the tenant period of site occupation between the middle 1860s and early 1900s.

Pig bones from the entire animal were recovered at the site, indicating that these animals were raised and butchered at the farm. Good quality meat cuts, such as hams and roasts, were eaten by the farm residents, in addition to less desirable portions, such as feet and head cuts. Archaeologists some-times view the consumption of less appetizing meat cuts at rural domestic sites as an indicator of poverty. However, it should also be emphasized that farm families as a rule often did not waste food, utilizing all edible parts of livestock. For example, farm families that raised pigs often humorously remarked that "everything except the squeal was used for food." Further, several rural cultural traditions, such as German-American and African-American folk foodways traditions, placed culinary value on seemingly less desirable meat cuts, such as feet and head portions. These cuts were used to prepare culturally distinctive dishes such as pig's feet and head cheese. Mini-mally, caution should be exercised regarding generalizations about rural foodways and socioeconomic class that are sometimes wielded by historical archaeologists, because it is easy to project our own food preferences and biases uncritically into the rural past. In addition to pork, beef and chicken were also eaten to a lesser extent at the farm. Only the bones from individual beef cuts were recovered at the site, and other elements, such as leg or head bones, were not recovered, indicating that cattle were probably not butch-ered at the farm but that individual cuts were purchased from a butcher.

The Shaeffer farm is archaeologically relevant because it illustrates mate-rial life at a Northern Appalachian farm during the antebellum period. The farm was operated by a large family that resided in a log house and had a noticeable taste for pork. These characteristics are prevalent among both Germans in western Pennsylvania and residents throughout Appalachia, perhaps illustrating the source of distinctive traits thought to be hallmarks of these overlapping culture regions. Further, the Shaeffer family belonged to the rural middle class, and this position is reflected in their use of fashion-able consumer items such as matching tableware and teaware. And although the family resided in a region of western Pennsylvania that experienced delayed frontier conditions, they were nonetheless quite aware of consumer trends occurring in popular culture.

In addition to these observations, the Shaeffer farm is also archaeologi-cally informative because it was occupied by farm owners during the first half of its occupation (ca. 1830–1864) and was inhabited by tenant farmers during the second half of its history (ca. 1864–1900). Consequently, the site offers the interesting opportunity to compare material conditions between these two rural tenure classes at one farm occupied during most of the 1800s. As mentioned previously, wealth enumerated in agricultural census records indicates that the Shaeffer family belonged to the rural middle class. Conversely, tenant farmers in Valley Township surrounding the Shaeffer farm were usually at the bottom of the rural economic ladder. Interestingly, however, material conditions revealed archaeologically during the two occupation periods at the site do not appear to have been drastically or noticeably different, and in fact a few unexpected trends are discernible.

For example, the distribution of ceramics by ware, decoration, and minimum vessel count suggests that the tenants during the second half of the farm's operation during the postbellum period were purchasing and discarding ceramics that were comparable in quality and quantity to the ceramics used by the Shaeffer family during the preceding antebellum era. Likewise, meat consumption at the site was noticeably consistent throughout its occupation. Last, Bedell and colleagues (Bedell et al. 1994: 53–54) note that the postbellum tenants were fairly active consumers, purchasing, breaking, and discarding the fragments of at least six different china dolls and numerous patent medicine bottles. And although the household items used by the tenants during the postbellum period at the farm were seemingly comparable to their predecessors and contemporary neighbors, the tenants at the farm did reside in a two-room log house. By the end of the Civil War, log dwellings were often viewed as old-fashioned or backward in many parts of the eastern United States. Consequently, household material consumption among tenants at the Shaeffer farm was probably not drastically different from their neighbors, yet their small and aging residence did perhaps denote their position within the surrounding rural hierarchy.

Multigenerational Material Life at the Gibbs Farmstead

The Nicholas Gibbs farmstead is located in Knox County, East Tennessee, near Knoxville. The site contains the original log house constructed about 1792 and the extant house lot. The farm was operated by four generations of the Gibbs family: Nicholas Gibbs (1792–1820), his son Daniel Gibbs (1821–1850), grandson Rufus Gibbs (1852–1905), and great-grandson John Gibbs (1905–1913). From 1913 to the 1980s the house was occupied by tenants who did not farm the surrounding land. The Gibbs site is a relevant example of a nineteenth-century middle-class farm in Southern Appalachia. Fairly aggressive commercial farmers, the site's residents practiced grain and livestock agriculture.

At one of the most intensively studied farmsteads in East Tennessee, excavations were conducted at the Nicholas Gibbs house between 1987 and

1996 by students with the historical archaeology program, Department of Anthropology, University of Tennessee, Knoxville, under the direction of Charles Faulkner (Faulkner 1988a, 1988b, 1989, 1991, 1992, 1998). The site was also, subsequently, the subject of dissertation research (Groover 1998, 2001, 2003, 2004, 2005). An early example of descendant group archaeology, fieldwork at the Gibbs house was initiated in 1987 by an invitation from the Nicholas Gibbs Historical Society to conduct excavations at the site. This society is composed mainly of Gibbs family descendants. It has maintained the Gibbs house and the acreage surrounding the house lot as a community museum since 1986.

The research design originally implemented at the Gibbs site in 1987 by Charles Faulkner focused on two main questions: reconstructing the farm lot's landscape history, particularly the period associated with Nicholas Gibbs, and defining the material culture associated with frontier-era German-American households in East Tennessee. Concerning landscape history, the Gibbs house is one of only a few surviving rural house lots and dwellings associated with original settlers in Knox County.

At the request of the Nicholas Gibbs Historical Society, a multiyear excavation program was initiated in 1987 to identify the previous locations of outbuildings in the inner house lot that were associated with the Nicholas Gibbs occupation of the residence. The historical society hoped to reconstruct the early outbuildings at a future date. To aid in reconstructing the immediate domestic landscape and identifying the locations of previous outbuildings, in 1987 Mrs. Ethel Gibbs Brown, the great-great-granddaughter of Nicholas Gibbs, was interviewed by anthropology student Marie Mathison (Brown 1987; Mathison 1987). The interview was conducted in conjunction with site excavation. In addition to providing important family history about the farmstead's built environment and domestic architecture, Mrs. Brown also sketched a detailed (and very accurate) memory map of the house lot as it appeared in the first decades of the twentieth century during her childhood (Figure 4.2). Her recollections and memory map were instrumental in interpreting the landscape history of the site and aptly illustrate the beneficial role that descendants can contribute to excavations at historic sites.

During the multiyear investigations at the Gibbs site, five blocks of units were excavated along the west and north perimeter of the house lot in a west-to-east, clockwise direction (Figure 4.3). The locations of the block excavations were selected based on information provided by Mrs. Brown. Excavation loci, designated Areas A, B, C, and D, were also selected based

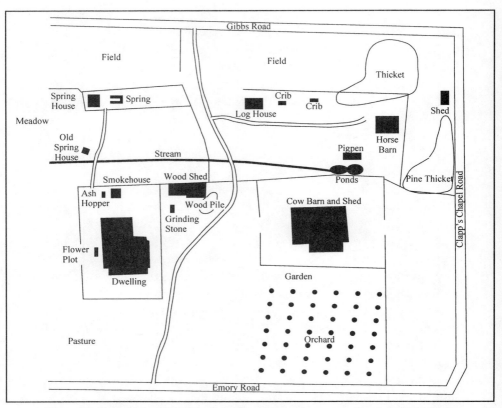

Figure 4.2. House lot at the Gibbs farm based on memory map drawn by Mrs. Ethel Gibbs Brown.

on visible topographic features in the rear house lot that appeared to be likely locations for structural remains associated with outbuildings. Area B, located in the western portion of the rear house lot, was selected first for archaeological testing. Subsequently in 1988, Area C, in the lot's upper northwest corner, was archaeologically sampled. Area D, located along the north edge of the rear yard, was excavated in 1989, 1990, and 1991.

The excavation strategy implemented in 1987 resulted in the discovery of the original smokehouse's location in 1989. Further, this effort produced substantial rewards. The most significant feature encountered archaeologically at the Gibbs site was a large pit cellar associated with the farm's original smokehouse. During the following year, in 1990, this pit cellar was fully excavated. In 1991, excavations were again resumed in Area D to locate the surrounding structural remains associated with the smokehouse that stood

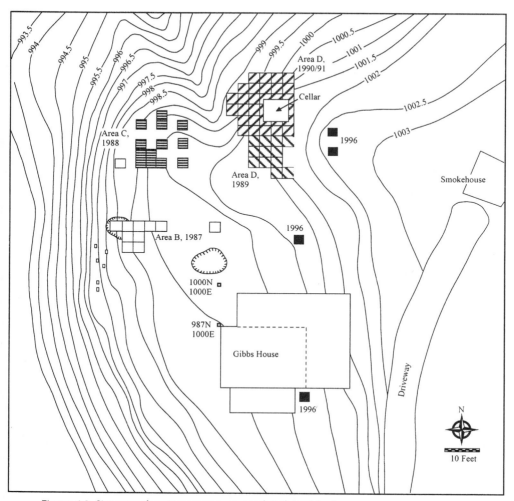

Figure 4.3. Site map showing areas excavated at the Gibbs farm.

over the pit cellar. Unfortunately, the foundation stones for the smokehouse had apparently been removed when the building was moved. Five years later, during the summer of 1996, a systematic shovel test survey was excavated over the entire house lot and three additional test units were also excavated.

The Gibbs site is important archaeologically because it illustrates several concepts useful to the interpretation of farmsteads, especially the influence of family life cycles upon landscape change and material consumption. Prevalent in sociology, rural history, and anthropology, the family life cycle refers to the life history of a household or extended family. As an extended family at a single farm waxes and wanes, it can significantly influence the domestic landscape, the dwelling, and household material consumption. Fortunately for archaeologists, household-level material consumption and discard exhibit cyclical behavior that in turn produces quantifiable and detectable correlates in the archaeological record. Research conducted at the Gibbs farm illustrates the influence of household cycles upon landscape change and material consumption (Groover 1998, 2001, 2003, 2004).

Based upon ideas developed by Goody (1978), the family cycle model used in the study of the Gibbs site divides the life cycle of the household into three simple yet analytically useful divisions, the young, mature, and old phases. These divisions can also be referred to interchangeably as early, middle, and late stages in the household cycle. The early phase of a household occurs when a couple begins to have children and starts a family. The mature or middle phase of the family life cycle, characterized by family fissioning, begins when the oldest mature children leave home and the family becomes smaller. The final period of the family life cycle is the late or old phase, which a family reaches when most or all of the children have left home and started their own households. A second household cycle can occur within a family when a grown son or daughter assumes household authority and operates the family's farm or plantation. During this stage a new family cycle begins, and retired parents often reside with the new household heads.

As illustrated at the Gibbs site (Figure 4.4), it is not uncommon for farms to have been inhabited by several biologically related, successive households. Contextually, multiple family cycles have elapsed at these sites, which in turn can potentially influence the archaeological record. Borrowing from genealogy and kinship terms, this situation is called a lineal family or a multigenerational family, denoting a direct family line from parents to offspring and later generations that specifically inhabited a site. The lineal family is considered to be different from the extended or collateral family, composed of more distant relations, such as cousins, aunts, or uncles, that never specifically resided at a given study site.

Archaeologically, the family cycle is an important systemic cultural-historical process that serves as a perpetual engine or catalyst for day-to-day motion and movement within the household. The household cycle influences the daily and long-term consumption of subsistence resources and the discard of material culture. Household succession, in which senior household members pass authority to junior members, is also an important

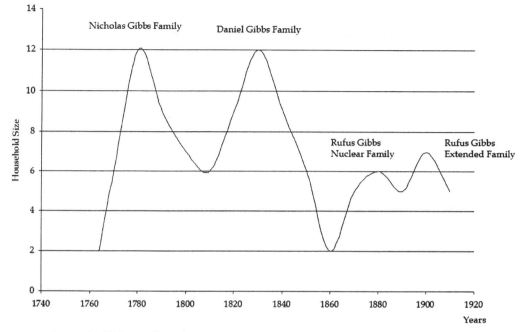

Figure 4.4 Gibbs family cycles.

source of household restructuring that can result in major site events and landscape change.

Archaeological investigations, unusually detailed family records, and information provided by informants helped to identify numerous examples of landscape change within the house lot that were associated with household succession at the Gibbs farmstead. Household succession at the farm occurred when a son in the family, such as Daniel (the second household head at the farm), inherited the farm from his father, Nicholas. For example, temporal shifts in the location of refuse disposal areas were defined at the Gibbs site (Figures 4.5 and 4.6).

Called midden shift (Groover 1998, 2003, 2004; Cabak and Groover 2004, 2006), the earliest material in the rear house lot, corresponding to the Nicholas Gibbs household, was lightly deposited on the periphery of the rear yard approximately 20 yards from the dwelling. Later, densely deposited material, dating after the 1820s through the remainder of the nineteenth century, was located immediately adjacent to the rear kitchen door of the dwelling. The Daniel and Rufus Gibbs households discarded this later material. The midden shift at the site was defined by excavating posthole test

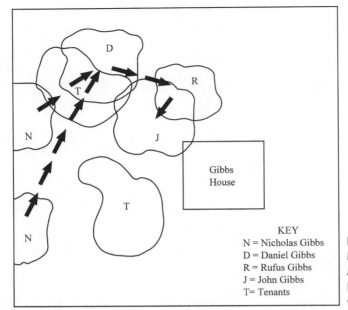

KEY
N = Nicholas Gibbs
D = Daniel Gibbs
R = Rufus Gibbs
J = John Gibbs
T= Tenants

Figure 4.5. Midden shift and associated households at the Gibbs farm.

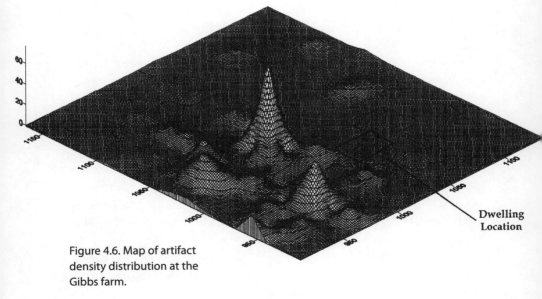

Dwelling Location

Figure 4.6. Map of artifact density distribution at the Gibbs farm.

pits within a formal site grid and calculating mean artifact dates (Cheek and Friedlander 1990; Groover 1998, 2003, 2004) for each test pit. The test pits were excavated with posthole diggers, as opposed to shovel test pits using shovels. The resulting dates were then plotted on a base map of the site and also compared to a wire frame artifact density map. Midden analysis indicates that over time among the Gibbs family, refuse disposal moved in a clockwise direction from west to east, shifting from the outer to the inner rear yard. Specific midden loci associated with individual households were also identified, including material deposited during the tenant period of site occupation.

The archaeologically defined shift in midden location and changes in refuse disposal practices at the Gibbs site also illustrate the archaeological concept of maintenance decline (Groover 1998, 2003, 2004; Cabak and Groover 2004, 2006). The original site residents at the Gibbs farmstead kept the immediate rear house lot free of refuse and discarded material on the edge of the lot. Conversely, later residents after the 1820s expended less effort in keeping the rear lot clean and discarded refuse immediately outside of the rear kitchen addition. This observable shift in refuse disposal practices after the 1820s, corresponding to household succession, resulted in a noticeable overall decline in the maintenance of the rear yard and a substantial increase in midden accumulation. Increasing levels of consumerism, especially during the second half of the nineteenth century, also encouraged maintenance decline and midden accumulation at the site. This trend is indicated on the wire frame map by the high density artifact locus associated with the Rufus Gibbs period of site occupation between 1852 and 1905 (Figure 4.6).

Besides midden shift and maintenance decline, changes in the location and function of outbuildings in the rear house lot were also identified at the Gibbs site. Shortly after settling the farmstead in 1792, Nicholas Gibbs constructed a log smokehouse. Located immediately behind the log dwelling, it contained a square-shaped pit cellar. This cellar was used for food storage until the early 1820s. During the 1820s, corresponding to the shift from the Nicholas Gibbs to the Daniel Gibbs occupation of the site, butchering and household refuse began to be deposited in the cellar. This activity continued until the early 1850s when the pit cellar was totally filled with material. Interestingly, the period in the early 1850s when the top of the cellar was capped corresponds to the transition between the Daniel Gibbs and Rufus Gibbs occupation of the site. Additional changes in outbuilding location again occurred at the beginning of the John Gibbs period of site occupation. In 1905, John Gibbs inherited the farmstead from his father, Rufus. A few

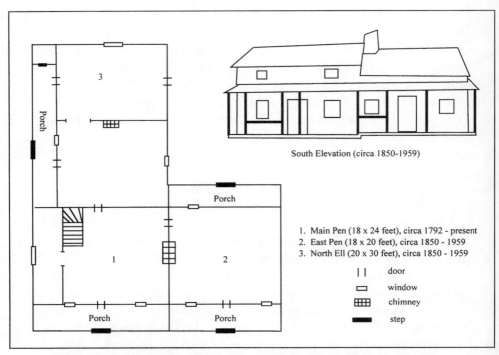

Figure 4.7. Map of the Gibbs house showing dwelling expansion over time corresponding to household succession events.

years later, John Gibbs moved the original log smokehouse to the east area of the house lot and constructed a new frame smokehouse near its former location.

In addition to shifts in the location of refuse deposits, maintenance decline within the house lot, and changes in outbuilding locations, several substantial expansion and renovation episodes also occurred to the dwelling that correspond to household transitions at the Gibbs farmstead. The original log dwelling was constructed in 1792. In the early 1850s, immediately before or after the death of Daniel Gibbs, when Rufus Gibbs assumed possession of the property from his father, Daniel, an east pen and north kitchen ell were added to the dwelling, significantly increasing its size (Figure 4.7). Further, a major dwelling renovation also occurred to the farmhouse in the early 1950s, after the death of John Gibbs in 1951, when Ethel Gibbs Brown, his daughter, inherited the property. At this time, Mrs. Brown had the kitchen ell and east pen, dating to the early 1850s, removed and replaced with new additions in the same locations. The house was also modernized at this time

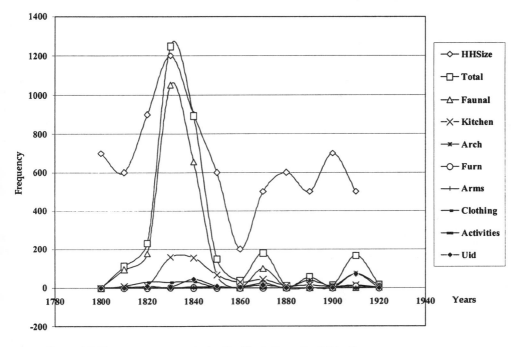

Figure 4.8. Time sequence analysis of artifacts from the Gibbs farm.

with the installation of electricity and running water. Later, in 1986, when the Nicholas Gibbs Historical Society assumed ownership of the property, society members removed a springhouse and conducted additional general repairs and renovations to the log dwelling and house lot.

Beyond landscape change, the family cycles and succession episodes at the Gibbs farmstead also influenced the daily and long-term consumption and deposition of specific types of artifacts. The influence of household cycles upon material consumption was identified through a new method called time sequence analysis (for a detailed discussion of the method see Groover 1998, 2001, 2003). This method involves the excavation and dating of thin arbitrary levels and subsequent analysis of artifacts by levels and generated artifact dates. At the Gibbs site, the archaeological results of time sequence analysis were compared to the actual household cycles of the Gibbs family, reconstructed from genealogical records.

As illustrated in Figure 4.8, the faunal and redware assemblages recovered from block excavations closely parallel the Gibbs household cycles, especially during the episode of site occupation associated with the Daniel Gibbs family. Although the relationship appears to diminish after 1860, nonetheless the faunal and redware assemblages produced significant statistical results, indicating that these two artifact categories were interrelated and undoubtedly influenced by household cycles. To determine if household cycles were influencing faunal consumption and redware use, the strength of the relationship between these variables was statistically measured using simple regression analysis. The regression results indicated that a strong relationship existed between household cycles, faunal consumption, and redware use. Simply put, the amount of redware and animal bones discarded at the site fluctuated over time according to the size of the Gibbs lineal family between the 1790s and the early 1900s.

Ceramic analysis results also indicated that the use and discard of hand-painted tableware and teaware also possessed a statistical relationship with the ebb and flow of the household cycles within the Gibbs lineal family (Figure 4.9). Translated to the archaeological record and the systemic context of the Gibbs household, the relationship between family cycles and the discard of painted ceramics further indicates and supports the idea of continuity initially suggested by the temporal persistence of redware and faunal resources. As illustrated by the analysis results of ceramic tableware, the Gibbs family members over time consistently selected similar decorative types, such as moderately priced painted wares, for most of the nineteenth century, in proportion to diachronic increases in family size. Perhaps owing to representing a combination of cost, personal preference, and the conservative character often attributed to vernacular folk cultures, the same basic, everyday ceramic assemblage was consistently used by each successive generation in the Gibbs family during most of the nineteenth century. Time sequence analysis, coupled with the concept of household cycles, effectively illustrates the persistence of this material tradition.

Beyond the influences of household cycles upon landscape change and material consumption, archaeology at the Gibbs site also illustrates cultural characteristics of a Southern Appalachian farmstead. The Gibbs family resided in a log house for over 100 years. The faunal remains from the Gibbs site indicate they preferred pork during their occupation of the site, with beef and chicken being consumed to a much lesser extent. Comprising over half of the ceramic sample from the site, the Gibbs family also relied heavily upon redware ceramics during the 1800s. Analysis of agricultural census records also indicate they were fairly aggressive grain and livestock farmers, raising a substantial amount of surplus farm products during most of the operation of the farm by the Gibbs family.

Paralleling a commercial farming orientation, the family members were

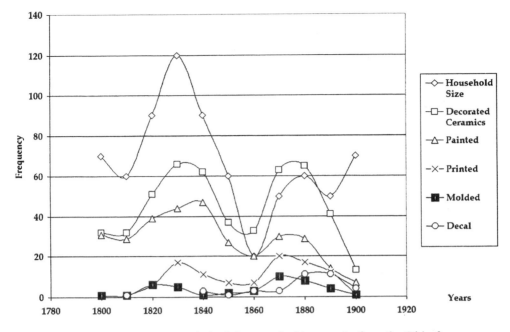

Figure 4.9. Time sequence analysis of decorated table ceramics from the Gibbs farm.

also active consumers, setting their dinner table with pewter plates (revealed by inventory analysis), and they also used a noticeable amount of transfer-printed ceramics, as revealed archaeologically. And although they enjoyed a comfortable standard of living, it appears that most of the profits from commercial farming was reinvested into land. Farmland was subsequently given to the children in the family as inheritance gifts when they came of age and started their own families. This economic strategy, designed to sustain the extended farm family, was successful for over a century, until the amount of land held by the family diminished due to partible, or equal, inheritance practices.

It is also relevant to note that many of the material characteristics identified at the Gibbs farm are noticeably similar to trends identified in the preceding discussion of the Northern Appalachian Shaeffer farm in western Pennsylvania. The Shaeffer family resided in a log house, practiced grain and livestock farming, and had a noticeable preference for pork, similar to the Gibbs family. It is tempting to state that these material characteristics illustrate an "Appalachian cultural pattern." Further complicating comparison of these two farms is the fact that both families were of German ancestry. The Gibbs family originated in England during the 1600s but migrated to Germany for religious reasons. Nicholas Gibbs, the family patriarch, grew up in Germany, spoke and wrote German, and also lived in Pennsylvania German areas of the Middle Atlantic during young adulthood before moving to the Lower South. When he moved to the Lower South from Maryland, he settled in a German enclave in Orange County, North Carolina, and married Mary Efland, a young lady from this community. Mary's family had likewise previously moved from the Pennsylvania German area of the Middle Atlantic region near where Nicholas Gibbs had formerly lived.

These interesting cultural and material parallels illustrate a relevant issue concerning interpretation in historical archaeology. Are the distinctive parallels identified at the Gibbs and Shaeffer farms owing to regional culture, ethnicity (such as their German ancestry), or a combination of these circumstances? To complicate matters, many regions of the United States, such as Appalachia, were settled by a broad range of people from different nationalities, ethnicities, and racial groups possessing distinctive cultural characteristics. However, it is often problematic to determine if defined material characteristics are unique or distinguishing for a given region, culture, racial group, or nationality.

For example, log dwellings, grain and livestock farming, and a preference for ham and pork chops appear to be prevalent rural cultural characteristics among both the residents of Appalachia and German immigrants, yet these traits are also widespread in the Midwest and Lower South. These characteristics are likewise found among both white and black rural residents of eastern North America. Consequently, can these traits realistically be used to define regional, ethnic, or racial traditions, or should these cultural characteristics perhaps best be viewed as prevalent, pan-regional cultural traits? The widespread distribution of cultural characteristics, their origins, diffusion, transformation, and the cultural traditions that they represent, are relevant interpretive issues in historical archaeology. As this brief example illustrates, however, teasing out cultural attributes and traditions at farmsteads can quickly become a complex process, one that is not amenable to simple answers. This is not a shortcoming of historical archaeology but illustrates an interesting challenge often confronted by researchers investigating rural material life.

The Midwest: The Transition to Commercial Agriculture at the Shepard Farm

Archaeological research conducted at the Shepard farm in Battle Creek, Michigan, illustrates material characteristics of the transition to commercial agriculture in the Midwest during the antebellum period. Part of a long-term research program focusing on the landscape history and archaeology of southwest Michigan (Rotman 1995; Rotman and Nassaney 1997; Nassaney et al. 2001), the Shepard farm has been the subject of intensive study by historical archaeologists at Western Michigan University (Nassaney 1998; Nassaney and Nickolai 1999; Sayers 1999, 2003; Sayers and Nassaney 1999). Archaeological excavations were conducted there in 1996 and 1998 to assist the Historical Society of Battle Creek in developing the extant brick Shepard farmhouse into an agricultural museum. Fieldwork consisted of remote sensing followed by site excavations. Remote sensing was conducted using magnetometry, electrical resistivity, and ground penetrating radar surveys. Approximately 120 units were then excavated, resulting in the identification of several midden locations, the discovery of numerous features, and the recovery of about 20,000 artifacts.

Following the completion of fieldwork, archaeological investigations at the Shepard farmstead were subsequently the basis of thesis research conducted by Daniel Sayers (1999, 2003). Drawing upon current debates among agricultural historians (e.g., Kulikoff 1992), Sayers explored how progressive farming and the developing commercial farming economy in the region influenced landscape change, household political economy, and the general material conditions experienced by the Shepard household. The archaeological study conducted by Sayers is significant because it presents a detailed example of the transition from frontier conditions to commercial farming in the Upper Midwest.

The farmstead was originally established by Warren Bronson Shepard, who moved from New York to Calhoun County, Michigan, in 1834 to teach school. Four years after moving to Battle Creek in Calhoun County, Shepard married Almeda Davis. The parents of seven children, Warren and Almeda were members of the First Baptist Church. Warren was a Democrat and also a member of the Freemasons. During the late 1830s, he taught school, was a brick manufacturer for a short period, and also operated a 120-acre farm with Almeda. Warren and Almeda's daughter Emily inherited the family farm and lived there until 1919. Shortly before her death, Emily sold the farm outside the family in 1925. During the remainder of the twentieth century, the brick farmhouse was occupied by a series of tenants and short-term owners until it was purchased by the Battle Creek Historical Society in 1990.

Prior to American settlement in the 1830s, the region surrounding Battle Creek and the Shepard farm in southwest Michigan was originally inhabited by the Potowatomi. Following the forced removal of Native Americans in the area, southwest Michigan began to be settled by pioneer farm families in the 1830s. Typical of frontier conditions, early settlers in the region practiced subsistence farming, relied upon kin-based reciprocal labor systems, and produced a wide range of household manufactures. The frontier farming economy in southwest Michigan initially focused upon grain and livestock agriculture. Kin-based labor consisted of agricultural labor provided by family members. Reciprocal labor, often called neighboring, was also a prevalent labor practice on the frontier where neighbors and community members pooled labor and helped one another with communal tasks, such as house raisings, barn raisings, planting, and harvests. Household manufactures were utilitarian, essential products that were made in the home, often by the women of the household, such as cloth and clothing, candles, or beeswax. Part of a barter economy, these economically valuable items were used by farm families and also traded at the local store for needed household items, such as sugar or salt, that farm families could not produce themselves. By the late 1840s and early 1850s, frontier conditions began to diminish in southwest Michigan. Home manufactures were declining by the 1850s, and commercial grain farming was increasing during the 1860s. This important transition from frontier conditions to commercial agriculture in southwest Michigan was also encouraged by the progressive farming movement in the Midwest.

The archaeological study of the Shepard farmstead illustrates in miniature how these larger trends that were active in the Upper Midwest—the superimposition of commercial, progressive farming upon an extant pre-progressive agricultural landscape—influenced material conditions and social relations within an antebellum farming household. During the 1830s the Shepard family endured frontier conditions. Constructed in 1834 on the summit of a Native American earthen mound, the family's residence was a log house located in the north quarter of the original 50-acre tract purchased by Warren Shepard (Figure 4.10). This original farm lot contained several outbuildings, and, perhaps reflecting the family's Irish pastoral heritage, they raised free-ranging cattle and sheep. During this time Almeda Shepard produced several types of home manufactures, consisting of can-

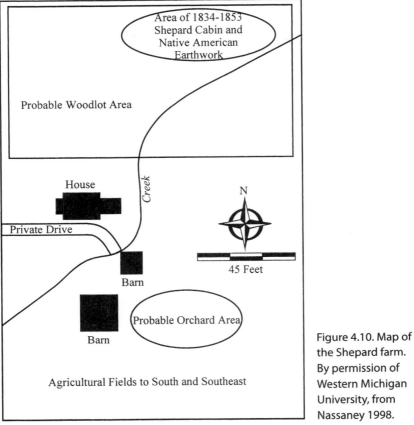

Figure 4.10. Map of the Shepard farm. By permission of Western Michigan University, from Nassaney 1998.

dles, clothing, and beeswax. Poultry and dairy products were also raised by the family.

By the middle 1840s, within approximately a decade after establishing the farm, the Shepard family began to aggressively transform their level of agricultural production and their related standard of living. Sayers (1999, 2003) emphasizes that the progressive farming movement was a primary catalyst for this transition at the Shepard farm. Prior to 1849, the family worked 50 improved acres. Between 1850 and 1860, 40 more improved acres were added to the farm's holdings (Table 4.1). Paralleling the expansion of their farming operations, the family subsequently moved out of their log house on top of the Indian mound and established a new, compact farm complex approximately 60 yards south of the original log dwelling. Between 1853 and 1854 the Shepard family constructed a two-story brick, Greek Revival

Table 4.1. Acreage at the Shepard Farm, 1834–1860

Year	Acreage Total
1834	79.15
1838	119.15
1843	119.15
1834–1849	50 improved acres total
1850–1860	100 improved acres total

house, a prevalent dwelling style used as a symbol of rural affluence among prosperous farm families. Containing a kitchen ell on the east side of the structure, the new brick dwelling was the centerpiece of the new farm lot. In 1856 a garden with a walkway was also created immediately east of the kitchen ell, and by 1858 two barns had been constructed immediately south of the brick dwelling (Figure 4.10).

Sayers (1999, 2003) emphasizes that the new 1850s complex established at the Shepard farm, containing outbuildings oriented along the side and rear of the domestic compound, conformed to the most prevalent type of nucleated farm lots promoted in progressive literature. This type of pre-planned design contrasted markedly with pre-progressive, vernacular-inspired frontier house lots, called a strewn house lot pattern by cultural geographers, in which the dwelling and related outbuildings appear to have been haphazardly scattered across the domestic landscape.

As the house lot and dwelling were relocated at the Shepard farm, the standard of living practiced by the farm residents, particularly revealed by foodways, was likewise influenced by popular consumer trends. The ceramic assemblage recovered from excavations indicates that during the antebellum occupation of the farm, the Shepard family used a combination of both cheaper and more expensive tableware. The less expensive ceramics, composed of Rockingham and annual wares, spanned the entire antebellum occupation period of the farm. The cheaper wares were probably used for food preparation and day-to-day kitchen activities. In contrast, the more expensive wares recovered from the site consisted of earlier ceramics dating to the 1830s and 1840s and later ceramics used during the 1850s and 1860s, after the family had moved to the new 1850s farm complex.

The earlier expensive tableware used at the site during the 1830s and 1840s, purchased before the family moved into the new 1850s lot but discarded in the new complex, included such specialty pieces as meat strainers, food serving vessels, and platters. Transfer-printed and hand-painted tablewares were also used during this period. The more expensive table service pieces recovered from excavations suggest that, despite the fact that lingering frontier conditions still prevailed in the surrounding region, the Shepard family was aware of fashionable dining trends and aspired to set a well-equipped dinner table. Interestingly, Sayers (2003) notes that the expensive ceramic fragments from this earlier period do not match. This discrepancy is mainly attributed to market availability: the Shepard family set a well-equipped table but was restricted to the tableware that was available from local merchants. Paralleling the move into the brick Greek Revival dwelling, the Shepard family purchased a matching set of Romantic Staffordshire transfer-printed table service in the Medici pattern. The set contained multiple vessel forms. The table service was also supplemented by the continued use of flowed, printed, and molded tableware in the Shepard household during the latter part of the antebellum period.

The ceramics recovered from archaeological excavations at the farm illustrate that the Shepard family was influenced by fashionable dining trends during the antebellum period. Conversely, faunal remains from the site suggest that a similar diet was practiced at the farm throughout the antebellum period, from the frontier era during the 1830s and 1840s and into the progressive period during the 1850s and 1860s. The Shepard family consumed mainly pork throughout their occupation of the farm. Moreover, typical of many farm households, butchering patterns indicate that practically all edible parts of the pig were consumed. This conservative, vernacular-based dietary practice is consistent with farm households, regardless of socioeconomic position, in which rural families do not waste food. Similar practices have been archaeologically documented at the middle-class Gibbs farm (Groover 1998, 2003), where pork was the predominant food for over a century and all parts of the animal were used. Similar dietary patterns have likewise been defined among enslaved households in the Lower South where meat cuts considered less desirable are prevalent in faunal assemblages (Reitz et al. 1985).

As a case study, the Shepard farm is informative because it illustrates the material details associated with the transition to commercial farming in the Midwest during the antebellum period. Perhaps most important, the Shepard farm underscores the fact that this significant juncture in the history of rural America was not a monolithic occurrence; rather, the adoption of commercial farming was a gradual, uneven, and complex process. Further, the culture change set in motion by commercial agriculture is often layered or cumulative and usually additive rather than subtractive. In the case of the Shepard farm, new elements were added to existing practices rather than existing practices being entirely replaced with new ways of doing things. Consequently, during periods of change and transformation, old practices continue, are modified, or intensify but are rarely discarded. Interestingly, this additive process in which new elements are layered upon previous practices, as Sayers illustrates (1999, 2003), can be a major source of ambiguity, contradiction, and potential tension within commercializing farm households.

For example, pre-progressive frontier households in the Midwest relied predominantly upon kin-based labor systems, where adolescent and adult family members were the main source of farm labor. Within this system, sons and daughters labored under delayed compensation, in which they were financially rewarded for their efforts through conveyance of land and dowries from their parents when they came of age and started their own families and farms. The system of delayed compensation was also a form of social control and a mechanism through which parents successfully appropriated labor from their progeny. In addition to kin-based labor, reciprocal labor practices were also used by neighbors and community members where tasks were completed by pooling labor between households.

The Shepard farm illustrates that commercial production gradually augmented pre-progressive, kin-based labor practices but never fully replaced them. In turn, this superimposition of old and new economic systems was undoubtedly a source of household contradiction, confusion, and tension when hired hands began to be used as a labor source on commercial or profit-oriented Midwest farms. At the Shepard farm, hired hands took meals with the family and were compensated for their labor mainly with foodstuffs and household manufactures, a type of use-value, barter-based exchange (Kulikoff 1992). Only in a few examples, as recorded in Warren Shepard's farm account ledger, were hired hands actually paid with cash. As a consequence, commercial agriculture for profit was being practiced at the Shepard farm by the 1850s and 1860s through the use of non-kin labor, but the hands were paid in a familial-like, reciprocal barter system. Moreover, they dined with the family during meals and also sat on the back porch and smoked tobacco pipes with Warren Shepard, as indicated by clay tobacco pipe concentrations in this area. Thus, the hired help were treated as family, or as fictive kin in anthropological terms, even though they were in reality paid help. Sayers (2003) emphasizes that this ambiguity, in which newly developing commercial-based exchange relations between non-family members were being grafted onto preexisting kin-based labor systems, served to obscure the economic and social reality active at this early commercializing farm. All said, the Shepard farm effectively illustrates the material contradictions inherent between progressive ideals, emphasizing commercial success and efficient use of the agricultural landscape, and the actual social realities of daily farm life during the antebellum period.

5

Postbellum and Twentieth-Century Farmsteads

During the first half of the nineteenth century, rural residents of America settled new farms, participated in expanding regional economies, and eventually enjoyed the benefits of newly created transportation systems, such as river travel and rail service. In turn, between the end of the Civil War and the first quarter of the twentieth century, from the 1860s to the 1920s, rural life in the United States also experienced several important transitions. These significant trends were related to changes in settlement patterns, the emancipation of slaves in the South and the expansion of tenant farming, the continued influence of industrialization and mechanization upon agriculture, and the effects of new technology and consumerism upon rural household life.

As illustrated in Figure 1.1, the number of farms dramatically expanded and contracted in the United States between the 1860s and 1920s. Following the Civil War, the number of farms continued to increase. Geographers call this settlement process infilling, in which the landscape becomes filled with occupants. In the South, rural infilling was encouraged by the emancipation of former slaves who subsequently established new farms after the Civil War. Likewise, in the Midwest, Plains, and West, settlers continued to inhabit new areas during the second half of the nineteenth century, encouraged by the opening of public lands and the influx of immigrants from eastern and western Europe. Rural infilling continued until the first quarter of the twentieth century, when, in 1920, 6.4 million farms were recorded by the U.S. Census of Agriculture.

After 1920, the number of farms continued to decline during the twentieth century, when the number leveled off and stabilized at 2.1 million, paralleling the number of farms in the 1860 census. The decrease in the number of farms during the first quarter of the twentieth century was the result of several interrelated factors. Similar to a hotel with no vacancies, as rural infilling continues in an area and the landscape becomes populated, it eventually reaches a maximum occupancy, where it is increasingly difficult for new farms to be established. In addition to the effect of infilling, farm consolidation also began to occur in the early twentieth century. With farm consolidation, the owners of larger, more prosperous farms often bought out smaller farms to increase the size of their landholdings. Farm consolidation resulted in a reduction in the number of farms, but the surviving farms often increased in size. Besides important population and economic factors, technology also played a major role in the reduction of the number of farms during the twentieth century. By the late 1800s and early 1900s, agricultural machines like the tractor began to replace human and animal labor. With the invention of more sophisticated gas-powered machinery, fewer people and fewer draft animals were required to work farms, especially larger, more commercially oriented operations.

Besides infilling and mechanization, advances in household technology and the influence of popular culture also materially transformed farm life and the built environment in rural settings during this period. Representing an architectural juncture from earlier periods, new house styles, such as Arts and Crafts inspired Craftsman dwellings, were marketed during the early twentieth century. Perhaps denoting a modern orientation to neighbors and the larger community, these new houses served as a visual statement, conveying the owner's identification with popular styles.

Modern household utilities and conveniences, such as electricity, plumbing, the telephone, and radio also dramatically altered daily life. The telephone and radio revolutionized communication, allowing isolated rural areas to become connected to the world beyond their doorsteps. Radio, magazines, and catalogs also influenced farm households by encouraging consumerism. During the early decades of the twentieth century, the popular idea of "modern" took hold among the public, and households began to actively adopt new practices, technology, and material culture. In this dynamic period, factory-produced consumer goods, ranging from household furnishings to clothing and personal items, became increasingly popular and affordable to larger segments of the rural population. Processed foods and name brands also became more prevalent as some farm families began to consume less of the food they raised and became more dependent upon grocery stores and retailers for basic household foodstuffs and supplies. Consumerism in rural areas was also encouraged by mail delivery and the establishment of mail-order retailers, such as the Sears and Roebuck Company. Likewise, the adoption of the automobile by larger numbers of rural households, especially after the 1930s, also increased the movement of goods and ideas and, in general, decreased the isolation that had typified rural life for much of its history in America.

All of these important historical trends consequently present unique but interesting challenges for historical archaeologists who encounter late-nine-teenth and twentieth-century farmsteads during fieldwork. For example, twentieth-century farmsteads are one of the most common types of archaeological sites in many parts of the country (Wilson 1990). Enhanced understanding of twentieth-century rural life is important because the small family farm has become a "unique institution of a simpler social order in which economic and domestic activities were inextricably bound together" (Friedberger 1988). Today, many family farms have been replaced by large commercial operations. This cultural and technological transformation of the family farm affected the majority of households in America and significantly restructured the primary production unit in the United States. Therefore, twentieth-century farm sites have the potential to provide important anthropological information about significant culture change within rural contexts. Effective evaluation of these resources is necessary because twentieth-century rural sites are numerous and their integrity is easily compromised by land development (Wilson 1990). This is especially a concern to federal land managers, like the Department of Defense, the U.S. National Forest Service, and the Bureau of Land Management, since these agencies typically manage large properties with thousands of twentieth-century sites.

From a perspective emphasizing medium duration time on the scale of centuries, farmsteads occupied during the late 1800s and into the twentieth century are also important archaeological resources because they represent the end of a substantial culture history sequence in American life. For example, if historical archaeologists want to address issues related to cultural continuity and change for sites occupied during the 1700s or early 1800s, then we must know what material life was like at sites occupied during the recent past. Simply put, we need to know what material elements persisted into the recent past that illustrate continuity, such as architectural styles or foodways traditions, to fully understand these characteristics during earlier periods, such as colonial or frontier situations. Similarly, in order to track material change, historical archaeologists must examine later periods, such as the late 1800s and into the first half of the 1900s. Ironically, these periods do not possess great time depth, but it is during these later periods that substantial culture change occurred.

Interestingly, historical archaeologists often address only issues related to short duration time at the level of a particular household or residence. This interval of time does not allow the identification of medium-term trends.

As a result, historical archaeology studies focusing upon principal historical trends that transpired over a period of medium-interval time (ca. 100 years or more) in a larger region are not often conducted. This fact is unfortunate because historical archaeologists have access to primary historical documents that would enhance the identification of important medium-interval temporal trends.

Temporal bias is also a negative by-product among studies that focus upon early sites falling within the range of short-duration time. Studies that implement a synchronic approach and rely upon the "earliest is best" strategy overlook or de-emphasize the full range of diachronic historical and cultural processes that unfolded from the beginning of settlement in a region until the recent past. Archaeologically, the medium-term history of America currently encompasses about a 500-year period, from the late 1400s to the 1950s. Based on cultural resource management laws, archaeological sites inhabited in the 1950s are the most recent resources that are potentially eligible for inclusion in the National Register of Historic Places. Consequently, important archaeological information related to later or more recent historical periods in North America, comprising the end of a substantial 500-year culture history sequence, is unknown or not yet fully explored. Conversely, when research questions are couched in scales of medium-interval time, then the information value of archaeological resources dating to the recent past, such as farmsteads occupied during the late 1800s and through the first half of the 1900s, can potentially become as important as the earliest archaeological sites in a region. Simply put, if the entire gamut of historical occupation in a study area is to be understood, then the full temporal range and material characteristics of sites in an area must be established, including both the earliest and most recent sites. With these thoughts in mind, the archaeological and information value of farmsteads occupied during the recent past is considered in this chapter.

Agricultural Expansion at the Porter Farm

The second half of the nineteenth century witnessed increasing levels of commercialization as prosperous rural households made the choice to expand their agricultural operations and provide farm surplus to local, regional, and national markets. Among rural households, the decision to engage more fully in commercial agriculture often had profound and long-term consequences. Previously raised crops and livestock were sometimes replaced with new regimes, landholdings increased over time, work relations in the family were modified, and material life in the household often became increasingly consumer-oriented. Site excavations conducted at the Lorren Porter farm in Chenango County, New York, illustrate material trends associated with commercial farming and upwardly mobile rural families during the second half of the nineteenth century in the Northeast.

The Lorren Porter farm site is located in southern New York State near the town of Coventry (Figure 1.2). The site, containing no above ground cultural features, was initially discovered and investigated in 1995 by archaeologists with the Public Archaeology Facility (PAF), State University of New York, Binghamton (Levendowski and Loren 1995; Levendowski and Versaggi 1995; Raffferty 1996, 2000). Site investigations at the Porter farm were part of a New York State Department of Transportation road improvement project. The historical archaeologists who originally located the Porter farm site recommended that as it was an important cultural resource, it should be the subject of data-recovery site excavations.

Archaeological data-recovery excavations conducted at the Porter farm were guided by several interrelated research questions. A central goal of the farm excavation was to use the site as a case study to illustrate the research potential of nineteenth-century rural residences. As discussed previously, farm sites during the 1980s and even the 1990s were often viewed by archaeological administrators and cultural resource managers as redundant information sources that contain little useful archaeological information. In contrast, during the past decade an increasing number of progressive-thinking archaeologists have recognized that farmstead archaeology is only limited by the research questions that we ask of this information source (e.g., Hart and Fisher 2000; Baugher and Klein 2003; DeCunzo 2004).

Inquiry at the Porter farm focused upon several related questions. Seán Rafferty (2000: 126–128) states that the site investigators were especially interested in using the Porter farm as an opportunity to critically evaluate the "Agrarian Myth," the long-held popular idea that farming represented an idyllic and sylvan way of life. Extolling the virtues of yeoman farmers, the Agrarian Myth had been espoused by our country's leaders, such as Thomas Jefferson, during the early 1800s. It was later adopted by the Populist political movement during the late 1800s. Among the Populists, farming illustrated a simple, pious, natural life, located away from the evils of the city, and farmers were viewed as the backbone of American democracy. The Populist movement occurred in reaction to increasing industrialization, urbanization, and associated culture change occurring during the late 1800s and early 1900s (Appleby 1982).

Historical archaeologists investigating the Porter farm wanted to use the site as a case study to illustrate that, in contrast to the Agrarian Myth, farm households during the early modern period were composed of complex individuals who often wanted to improve their economic situation, were economically enmeshed in intricate commercial systems located beyond their front porches, and were often acquisitive with regard to consumer culture and the standard of living they practiced. In addition to questioning the Agrarian Myth, archaeologists at the Porter farm also explored several supporting research questions, consisting of nineteenth-century social dynamics, changes in farming practices, changes in household production activities, and the development of consumer behavior in rural settings.

The social structure of rural New York State during the 1800s consisted of wealthy landowners, well-to-do farmers, skilled rural tradespersons, merchants, tenant farmers, and unskilled laborers. Assembled historical information indicates the site was first occupied by the Porter family in the 1840s. During the 1850s the Porter family was part of the rural middle class in Chenango County, based on farm value and production recorded in agriculture census returns. By the later decades of the 1800s, the family became members of the rural upper-middle class in the study region, corresponding to the period between the 1850s and early 1900s when agricultural practices on the Porter farm shifted from general mixed grain and livestock farming to commercial dairying, a capital-intensive farm regime.

The historical trajectory of the Porter farm illustrates the economic priorities and material choices of progressive, market-oriented farm families during the second half of the 1800s in the Northeast. In 1850 the Porter family consisted of household head Lorren (age fifty), his wife Eliza (age forty-four), and their children Charles (fifteen), Lucy (eleven), Sarah (nine), and Edward (seven). During the third quarter of the nineteenth century, mixed farming was practiced at the farm, and the Porter family raised grain (wheat, buckwheat, corn, and oats) and livestock (cattle, pigs, sheep, and poultry). In 1850 Lorren Porter's assets were $2,000, twice the average of his neighbors, and during the second half of the 1800s the size and value of the farm steadily increased, illustrating the deepening of commercial agriculture at the study site. During this period of commercialization in the last quarter of the 1800s, the farm became a medium- to large-sized commercial dairying operation. Dairying was supplemented with poultry, syrup, and orchard products raised by the family members. Eventually, Lorren Porter, the head of the household, sold the family farm to his son Charles in 1885, and Lorren died a short time later.

The artifacts recovered from site excavations serve to contextualize the known economic history of the farm residents, illustrate the daily material life experienced by the study family, and highlight the increasing consumerism that transpired at the farm. A 6 percent sample of the house lot was excavated during data recovery investigations, resulting in the exposure of 30 square meters of excavation area. During excavations a large sheet midden surrounding the dwelling was encountered, and one feature, a segment of a wall associated with the dwelling's foundation, was also identified. The resulting artifacts were used to conduct spatial analysis, examine distinct occupation episodes, explore consumerism and production at the farm, and address ceramic use among the site residents.

The domestic midden surrounding the dwelling was spatially and temporally distinct. Artifact chronology indicates that the midden on the west half of the house lot was created by the Lorren Porter household during the third quarter of the 1800s. Conversely, artifact deposits on the east half of the house lot dated to the Charles Porter period of site occupation during the last quarter of the 1800s (Figure 5.1). Called midden shift and discussed previously in Chapter 4 on the Gibbs farmstead (Groover 1998, 2003, 2004), this distinctive spatial pattern often occurs during episodes of household succession, when new heads of households (including new wives) assume authority in a dwelling. Perhaps as a means of expressing authority and decision-making, when succession occurs, new heads of households will often create new landscape-use patterns that are evident in landscape analysis, such as the use of different refuse disposal areas, as occurred at the Porter farm. The addition of a new wife or husband to the existing household would also contribute to midden shift and landscape change, such as dwelling alterations, since the new household member would not always be aware of or conform to previous landscape-use patterns, such as refuse disposal areas. Likewise, junior household members, when they came of age and assumed ownership and management of the family farm, also undoubtedly altered the existing landscape, with landscape changes such as moving outbuildings, fence lines, and work areas. As identified through spatial analysis, this same process occurred at the Porter farm.

The results of spatial analysis at the Porter farm allowed the separation of artifacts into distinct time periods corresponding to specific households. Comparison of the Lorren and Charles Porter assemblages consequently allowed the identification of diachronic material trends within the lineal family. Overall, increasing consumerism and material discard was evident

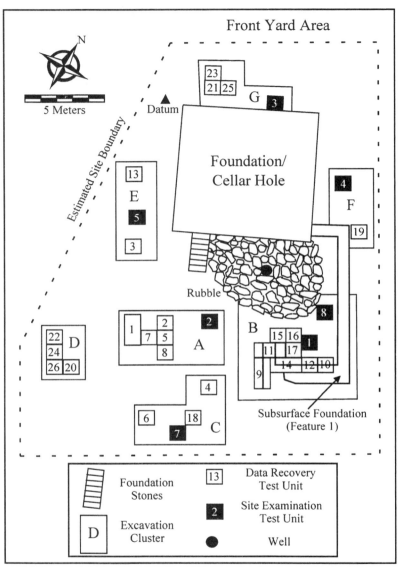

Figure 5.1. Map of the Porter farm showing midden locations. By permission of the New York State Museum, Albany, from Rafferty 2000, Figure 9.3, p. 130.

over time, although the Lorren Porter household was relatively acquisitive from the beginning of site occupation, as revealed by ceramic artifacts.

During the Lorren Porter occupation period, material was deposited on the west half of the house lot (Areas A, D, and E). A moderately dense midden dating to the 1850s encountered immediately south of the dwelling's rear wall contained a dense concentration of food remains. Material dating to this period included transfer-printed ceramics in high proportions, table- and teawares, and redware ceramics for food preparation and storage. The vessels in the ceramic assemblage were expensive, but the ceramic sample exhibited low vessel form diversity. The ceramic information suggests that the family purchased noticeably expensive transfer-printed ceramics in a limited range of vessel forms, mainly plates, teacups, and saucers. Interestingly, the transfer-printed ceramics were not vessels from matching sets, suggesting the family acquired nonmatching vessels from local merchants as needed.

This distinctive pattern of transfer-printed ceramic acquisition has been documented at other rural sites, such as the Gibbs farmstead in East Tennessee (Groover 1998, 2003, 2005; Chapter 4, this volume) and Bush Hill Plantation in western South Carolina (Cabak and Groover 2004, 2006). In both examples, transfer-printed tableware was harmonized or matched according to "color sets," such as deep blue table forms, but there were not any actual "pattern sets" identified on the transfer-printed vessels from the sites. The prevalence of color sets at rural sites suggests rural residents often matched the transfer-printed vessel colors during separate purchases of specific vessels, but they did not usually have matching sets composed of the same printed patterns. Simply put, among rural households at midcentury, the colors of their transfer-printed tableware often matched, but the printed patterns were different. This recurring ceramic-use pattern suggests rural residents had a distinctive attitude and consumer grammar or set of rules toward ceramic purchases: They were apparently concerned about the colors matching, but it was not important whether the transfer-print patterns themselves matched, possibly because they could not acquire matching sets. Consequently, this apparently widespread rural trend may have been a product of ceramic supply and was in part owing to the availability of tableware and individual transfer-printed vessels among country storekeepers.

Compared to five other contemporaneous domestic sites in New York State (the Keith farm, the Burghardt tannery owners, the Burghardt tannery workers, the Stower property, and the Mather property), Rafferty (2000:

139) notes that the Porter family had an appreciably high amount of transfer-printed ceramics but an average proportion of tableware and teaware
vessels. Consequently, the Porter family had a similar range of vessels compared to other domestic sites but had a noticeably larger amount of expensive ceramics. Interestingly, the Porter household used twice the amount of
food preparation and storage vessels compared to the five other nineteenth-
century sites. The large amount of preparation and storage vessels may have
been owing to the commercial dairying conducted at the farm.

Although expensive transfer-printed tableware was used during the Lorren Porter period of site occupation, Lorren's son, Charles, exhibited different consumer habits and refuse disposal behavior. During the Charles
Porter period of site occupation, the household midden shifted from the
west half of the house lot to the east half of the house lot (Areas B, C, and
F). Likewise, a dense midden was created immediately adjacent to the rear
wall of the dwelling. Overall, the Charles Porter midden on the east half of
the house lot contained more artifacts that were less expensive than items
used during the first half of site occupation. Simply put, compared to his
father, Charles consumed and discarded greater amounts of less expensive items, such as plain tableware. The later period of site occupation was
also characterized by greater amounts of glass containers and decreasing
amounts of food preparation and storage containers. These artifact trends
indicate that the farm residents during the 1870s and later were purchasing
more processed food items from merchants rather than consuming their
own foodstuffs. The decrease in food-processing artifacts also illustrates
how increasing farm commercialization encouraged consumerism and the
decline of household self-sufficiency. Apparently, the residents decided it
was more desirable or convenient to purchase food as groceries than process
their own food products. Further, the increasing use of groceries may have
been needed as fewer food items were raised on the farm, again a potential
by-product of farm commercialization and specialization.

In summary, the Porter farm underscores the fact that many farm families during the second half of the nineteenth century attempted to improve
their economic situation and at the same time actively adopted consumerism prevalent during the era. The Porter farm likewise illustrates the use-
fulness of multigenerational analyses in which shifts in consumerism and
purchasing preferences are tracked within a lineal household over time.
Consumerism at the farm reveals the idiosyncratic character and complexity of individual decision-making in families. These trends also emphasize
that archaeological expectations are not monolithic—one household may

value transfer-printed flatware and the succeeding family may place little value on expensive tableware. Likewise, different households made noticeably different consumer decisions that may have been influenced by gender, race, ethnicity, and socioeconomic class. And although the homogenization of material culture due to industrialization is apparent at farmsteads, households are often quite distinct from one another regarding consumption choices. The challenge for historical archaeologists is to identify and interpret these interesting details of rural life preserved in the material record.

Modernizing Farms along the Savannah River Valley

The middle Savannah River valley is located in western South Carolina and eastern Georgia near Augusta (Figure 1.2). This area of the state is a sub-region of the larger Sandhills of South Carolina. The Sandhills, an ancient ocean shoreline, extend across the state and separate the Piedmont from the Upper Coastal Plain (Kovacik and Winberry 1987: 18). Personnel with the University of South Carolina's Savannah River Archaeological Research Program have conducted farmstead and plantation archaeology in the middle Savannah River valley since the 1980s (Crass and Brooks 1995; Cabak and Inkrot 1997; Cabak et al. 1999; Brooks et al. 2000; Cabak and Groover 2004, 2006).

The economic history of the Savannah River valley can be divided into two broad periods, the agricultural era and the industrial/service era. During the former era, agriculture formed the foundation of the region's economy during the colonial, antebellum, and postbellum periods. During the colonial period, small subsistence farms were established by settlers, beginning in the 1730s. These early farms were later replaced with cotton plantations, encouraged by the adoption of the cotton gin in the 1790s. After the Civil War, cotton production continued under the tenancy system. The tenant system persisted until the second half of the twentieth century in the study area. However, after the 1950s the importance of agriculture began to decline in the Savannah River valley as the manufacturing and service sector began to develop. Today, agriculture forms a small part of the area's economy.

To better understand rural material life and the interpretive potential of these archaeological resources, farmsteads inhabited between approximately 1875 and 1950 in the middle Savannah River valley are considered through the interpretive concept of rural modernization. Farm modernization is investigated as both a historical process that transpired in the defined study region and a theoretical model that is considered potentially useful as an interpretive framework for late nineteenth- and twentieth-century farm sites across the United States.

Modernization is a cultural-historical process that contributed to the transition from pre-industrial, agrarian-based societies to industrial- and postindustrial-based societies throughout the world. Modernization is appropriate for historical archaeology as it contains a strong material and technological orientation. Essentially Cold War–era political policy, modernization theory was created by development scholars in the 1950s and 1960s. Its original purpose was to transplant Western, capitalist-based commercial economies to non-Western, developing regions of the globe, particularly Third World countries that might be susceptible to communism (Rostow 1960; Levy 1967; Preston 1982; Sanderson 1995). The original theory was ethnocentric and created false dichotomies between traditional and modern societies, rich and poor nations, and primitive and advanced cultures. Since the 1960s, modernization theory has been reformulated and today is seen to be the result of technological, agricultural, and industrial forces, including urbanization (Haviland 1994: 658–659). Contemporary scholars typically examine the intertwined relationship between tradition and modernity and specific historical processes associated with individual situations and contexts.

Scholars have demonstrated that modernization occurs differently throughout the world. Likewise, farm modernization has followed multiple paths of development. America was clearly an urban culture by the late nineteenth century, but the farming regions did not develop evenly—agricultural transformation occurred at uneven rates throughout the United States. America is presumed to have been a modern society of mass consumers by the 1920s, but specific subcultures or regions within the country modernized at different tempos. These fluctuations are not merely a result of single causes such as geographically specific crops or environments; rather, historical change is usually the result of complex interplay among numerous variables. Consequently, despite inherent shortcomings, the modernization model possesses the potential to provide insight into the interpretive interface between regional development, the adoption of new technology and crop regimes, the organization of class structure and gender roles at the community and household levels, and the general way that material culture change has transpired over the past 150 years in rural settings. Interestingly, previous studies that address these topics illustrate that historical change often does not transpire uniformly, but rather change occurs first in one domain and transformation can severely lag in other spheres of daily life.

For example, modernization could significantly influence gender roles within the domestic life of farm families and agricultural production. Within the home, labor-saving devices and the purchase of prepared foods would have potentially decreased the amount of labor that farm wives formerly devoted to household tasks. Likewise, as farms adopted new production technology, household manufactures conducted by women as supplemental income were sometimes appropriated by men within the household, displacing women from traditional income-earning farm activities. Illustrating this occurrence, McMurry (1995) historically documented the transition from women-centered dairying to male-centered commercial dairying in New England during the nineteenth century.

A modernization perspective is advocated as a productive framework for interpreting the continuum from traditional to modern farm life in North America, particularly for rural studies that examine the period after the Civil War. Two functional aspects of farm modernization lend themselves well to architectural and archaeological analysis. The first aspect of modernization particularly well suited to archaeological analysis is industrialization that resulted in standardized production, a veritable explosion of manufactured items, and mass consumption. A second advantage of modernization is the substantial amount of technological development that influenced both the domestic and work spheres. These two material components of modernization—industrialization and new technology—fortunately possess clearly definable and discernible archaeological characteristics.

Concerning the advent of consumer culture, modernization has exerted a homogenizing influence. As a society becomes more industrial, material culture becomes more similar (So 1990). For example, archaeologists have argued that the "cultural values, practices, and aesthetics" of consumerism during the Victorian period were a "homogenizing force" for the multiethnic population of the United States (Hardesty 1980). This process replaced traditional mores with modern values. Similarly, economist Thorstein Veblen developed a theory of conspicuous consumption in the late nineteenth century, maintaining that humans need to validate wealth, status, and personal social value through obvious display of material consumption (Veblen 1973). Industrial production coupled with conspicuous consumption and Victorian values led to the development of present-day consumer culture. Industrial goods are an indicator of mass consumption. Artifacts recovered from late nineteenth and early twentieth century farmsteads should in turn reflect how these larger material trends influenced daily life among rural households.

Technological developments associated with mechanization directly transformed farm operations and rural production and indirectly changed rural social organization (McClelland 1997). Mechanized farm machinery and scientifically based fertilizers and chemicals all produced larger crop yields. The mechanization of farm operations is often indicated by the archaeological recovery of tools or machinery parts. This mechanization also resulted in a surplus farm population, which eventually encouraged rural out-migration. Electricity and automobiles provided rural residents with the same access to popular culture as the rest of the nation. People consumed more processed foods (visible archaeologically by a decrease in food storage containers) and had access to popular entertainment such as movies and television. Faraway places were rendered more accessible via improved transportation technology. Architectural data likewise reveal characteristics about the built environment and provide information concerning the range of new technology adopted by farm households. For example, archaeological excavations typically recover artifacts related to domestic improvements, such as electrical hardware or new and improved construction materials that are indicative of modernization in the rural domestic setting.

The concept of the modern era crystallized collectively during the late nineteenth and early twentieth centuries. In the material domain, the influence of modernity and modernism was expressed in ideas emphasizing new technology, progress, and national infatuation with labor-saving consumer goods (Pursell 2001). Popular ideologies associated with the modern era that rejected traditionalism were also expressed in art, architecture, and decorative trends, such the Arts and Crafts movement and the Art Deco style, both of which are considered to represent the first modern design movements (Denker 1996; Hillier and Escritt 1997). Besides trends in popular culture, farm technology also substantially influenced and restructured rural life in the late nineteenth and early twentieth centuries. Many rural historians emphasize that this period was a critical juncture in terms of the technological change that occurred in agriculture (Fite 1981; Wright 1986; Adams 1993; Woodman 1997; Kleinegger 2001).

The number of Americans living on farms began to decrease between the late nineteenth and mid-twentieth century. Not only were the population characteristics of rural areas rapidly changing in the first half of the twentieth century, but farm life itself was restructured by technological and biological innovations. In fact, "the farmer," as a writer in the magazine *For-*

tune explained, was quickly becoming "more of an industrialist and farming was more a way to make a living than a mode of life" (Fite 1981: 77).

Although the United States was rapidly becoming an urban nation in the early twentieth century, rural communities remained an important aspect of life in the South. Two-thirds of southerners were still classified as rural in 1930, while only 25 percent of the nation's total population lived on a farm at this time (Terrill and Hirsch 1978: 41). Historians and geographers emphasize that as southern farms mechanized between the 1930s and 1960s, large numbers of southerners began to migrate from rural areas (Fite 1984: xii). Within a generation after World War II, southern commercial farms, according to scholars, could no longer be distinguished from farms in other parts of the country, except in the regionally specific crops they grew. Southern commercial farms, according to historians, were highly capitalized and mechanized. After 1945, the rural poverty that had characterized the region since the Civil War was disappearing, and journalists described "the New South as a place of opportunity" (Kovacik and Winberry 1987: 133).

Farmstead data illustrating modernization trends during the postbellum period were drawn from the Savannah River Site, located within the middle Savannah River valley of South Carolina. The soils in the area are generally considered to have low agricultural potential. Life along the Savannah River, until the past half century, was primarily agrarian, and most people earned their living from agriculture whether they lived on a farm or in town. After the Civil War, the tenant system became established and dominated agricultural practices. Two-thirds of the farmers in the study area were tenants, and most tenants were sharecroppers rather than cash renters. Farms were typically small in size and operated by the landowners or one or two tenant households. Reflecting the end of the agricultural era in the study area, by 1950 rural population and tenancy were decreasing in the middle Savannah River valley as industrial and service sector occupations became established.

Farmstead information was obtained from a random sample of the 1951 farms located on the Savannah River Site. The farms were all purchased by the federal government to establish a nuclear research facility. When the government purchased the properties from landowners in 1951, they measured, described, assessed, and photographed all the structures located on the tracts before they were razed or moved out of the area. Archival information was analyzed from 59 tracts that were randomly selected. The dwellings on 27 of these tracts were investigated archaeologically through limited site survey and testing. The archaeological sites were tested with 20 to 30 shovel test pits. The testing strategies focused on the inner yard surrounding the dwelling (Cabak and Inkrot 1997; Cabak et al. 1999).

The influence of the modernization process on the domestic setting at farmsteads was illustrated by the assembled archaeological and historical information. Modernization typically replaces folk culture with scientifically based knowledge and results in the mass consumption of industrially produced goods. Given that these changes usually accompanied modernization, it was anticipated that farm dwellings, particularly architectural styles, should reflect rural modernization as it relates to mass consumption. Analysis of the archaeological record can also potentially illustrate whether folk knowledge or cultural practices in the study area were influenced by consumerism and other trends prevalent in popular culture and household goods.

According to architectural historians, there are two basic categories of houses, folk and styled dwellings. Folk dwellings are considered to be "designed without a conscious attempt to mimic current fashion," whereas styled domestic architecture shows "the influence of shapes, materials, detailing, or other features that make up an architectural style that was currently in vogue" (McAlester and McAlester 1984: 5). The sample of Savannah River farmsteads revealed both the recent influence of national-level, popular culture in the area of domestic architecture and the persistence of earlier folk dwelling styles. Photographic documentation indicates that the dwelling sample contains nine architectural styles (Table 5.1). With the exception of the Craftsman, all dwelling styles are examples of folk houses. The Craftsman form represents a modern-style dwelling popular between about 1905 and 1930. Modern styles represent a scant 5 percent of all identifiable dwellings in the study sample. Apparently, the majority of rural residents in the middle Savannah River valley were little influenced by popular culture, at least in terms of the housing styles they chose to live in.

Concerning the persistence of folk houses in the study area, three of the vernacular styles possess substantial time depth in the South. The I-house is a folk style with British and colonial origins (Figure 5.2) (Wilson 1975; McAlester and McAlester 1984; Jakle et al. 1989). The hall-and-parlor house was popular between about 1750 and 1890 but persisted in the South well into the twentieth century (Forman 1948; McAlester and McAlester 1984). The Cumberland house (Figure 5.3), although popular between 1880 and 1920, is believed to represent a frame version of an earlier log dwelling form and therefore is considered to be a vernacular style (Jurney et al. 1988; Morgan 1990). Two folk styles, the shotgun and side-gabled, were typically built

Table 5.1. Distribution of Dwelling Styles at Farmsteads in the Middle Savannah River Valley in 1951 by Tenure Class

| | Farm Operator/Owner | | Tenant | |
Style	n	%	n	%
Craftsman	3	10.00	0	0
Cross Gable	2	6.70	0	0
Cumberland	3	10.00	10	30.30
Gable Front	1	3.30	0	0
Hall-and-Parlor	8	26.60	22	66.70
I-House	2	6.70	0	0
Shot Gun	3	10.00	0	0
Side-Gabled	6	20.00	0	0
Southern Bungalow	2	6.70	1	3.00
Total	30	100.0	33	100.0

Source: Cabak and Inkrot 1997: 103.

Figure 5.2. I-house near the Savannah River. By permission of the U.S. Department of Energy, from Cabak and Inkrot 1997, Figure 6.12, p. 106.

Figure 5.3. Cumberland dwelling near the Savannah River. By permission of the U.S. Department of Energy, from Cabak and Inkrot 1997, Figure 6.11, p. 105.

between the mid-nineteenth century and the early twentieth century (Vlach 1976; McAlester and McAlester 1984: 90, 98; Schlereth 1992: 89). These styles are considered to be transitional forms. Three folk styles, the southern bungalow, front-gabled, and cross-gabled, became popular in the South in the early twentieth century (McAlester and McAlester 1984: 90; Jakle et al. 1989: 143). The newer folk styles, as well as the Craftsman (Figure 5.4), are considered to be more modern dwelling forms than the other earlier or classic folk styles.

Although the older or classic vernacular-styled homes are indeed the most prevalent dwelling form in the dwelling sample, assembled photographs did not reveal if these folk-style homes were built in the twentieth century or if they are remnants from earlier periods. Archaeological information clearly demonstrates that the earliest folk styles continued to be constructed well into the twentieth century in the study area. Calcula-

Figure 5.4. Craftsman dwelling near the Savannah River. By permission of the U.S. Department of Energy, from Cabak and Inkrot 1997, Figure 6.20, p. 112.

tions were made to determine if modern-styled homes were more prevalent among wealthier farms. As expected, four out of five farm tracts with the highest monetary value contained the most modern-styled homes in the study area. The older I-house form was the exception, thus indicating that this vernacular style continued to be associated with rural affluence into the twentieth century. The smaller-sized and older-styled hall-and-parlor and Cumberland dwellings were consistently associated with lower property values. Housing style was clearly used as a form of social differentiation by the wealthy in the study area, and capital, in turn, was obviously a requisite for farm modernization.

To measure the extent of farm modernization revealed through the built environment, the farmsteads in the study sample were placed in etic analysis categories corresponding to what may have been considered modern in 1950. These categories consist of modern, transitional, and traditional farmsteads (Ahlman 1996). A fourth group was established for unidentified farmsteads. The characteristics of the three farmstead types are considered to be specific to the study area. Each farmstead in the study sample was placed into these etic categories for purposes of measuring the level of farm modernization. It appears that traditional, folk-style farmhouses dominated the agricultural landscape in 1950.

Despite the traditional nature of the farmsteads in the middle Savannah River valley, all of the communities in the region had access to mass-produced industrial goods by the late nineteenth century. Scholars emphasize that between the Civil War and World War II, U.S. households shifted from production to consumption, and the consumer culture that typifies life today gained momentum (Glickman 1999; Williams 2006). Archaeological data were used to explore when this fundamental juncture occurred within the rural domestic setting in the middle Savannah River valley.

Specific artifact types were examined to determine if this same level of cultural conservatism that influenced architectural styles also influenced the use of household goods and portable material culture. A wide range of artifact types could potentially provide sensitive information about the household-level adoption of modern technologies in the study area, such as light bulb sockets, spark plugs, and utility line insulators. Interestingly, none of the sites in this study produced these types of artifacts. The dearth of artifacts indicative of modern conveniences may be a result of the limited testing that was conducted. However, excavations conducted at Millwood Plantation (Orser 1988a), located north of the Savannah River Site, also provided scant evidence of rural utilities. Paralleling the conspicuous absence of electrical hardware from the sites, government records indicate that only a few homes and outbuildings in the study area contained modern construction materials. Likewise, few fragments of twentieth-century construction, such as concrete or asbestos, were found,

In addition to household utilities, historic studies indicate that items produced by the nation's expanding factories were available to rural communities by the twentieth century. Artifact types may be able to indicate when residents in the study area became immersed in national-level popular culture. Like electrical hardware, however, the sampled yard middens produced few artifacts that could be specifically associated with twentieth-century popular culture. Therefore, the following analysis is limited to a discussion of food storage technology, phonograph records, and soda pop bottles. These artifacts provide general insight into rural consumption habits and the spread of consumerism in rural contexts rather than indicating whether particular residents drank soda pop or listened to phonograph records.

Beginning in the early twentieth century, advances in food processing, refrigeration, and preservation, in combination with the new nutrition practices advocated by scientists, brought about major changes in rural foodways. During this time, stoneware jars were replaced by glass canning jars as a less expensive and more effective long-term food storage container. The presence of glass food containers can also indicate that farm inhabitants were consuming more commercially prepared foods.

Did the differences between modern and traditional farmsteads have an effect upon the distribution of stoneware at the study sites? It would be expected that modern farmsteads would have a lower proportion of stoneware if residents were changing their foodways earlier than the residents of more traditional farmsteads. However, since modern farmsteads have shorter occupations, relatively few sites should have stoneware, owing to the fact that glass replaced this ceramic in the twentieth century. Therefore, only the proportion of stoneware at the traditional and modern sites occupied between 1900 and 1950 was compared, to eliminate those sites that were occupied during the periods of heavy stoneware use. Eighteen percent of the traditional sites contained stoneware, as did 20 percent of the modern sites. Farm families thus began to change their foodways at approximately the same time, regardless of domestic modernization.

Concerning leisure-time activities that were dependent upon modern technology, subsurface testing recovered phonograph record fragments at three traditional farmsteads and one at an unidentified farmstead type. The extensive excavations conducted at Millwood Plantation did not recover record fragments (Orser 1988a). In addition to artifacts associated with recreation activities, glass soda bottle fragments were found in shovel test pits at 50 percent of the modern, 30 percent of the transitional, and 44 percent of the traditional farmsteads. Ayers (1992: 102), a historian, notes that "new innovations such as Coca-Cola pulled more people to southern stores more often." In turn, increased visits to stores undoubtedly resulted in more consumerism.

In summary, the results of the rural modernization study produced contrasting yet informative results. Consideration of the built environment at farmsteads in South Carolina's middle Savannah River valley illustrates the uneven character of rural development during the first half of the twentieth century. Within the domain of domestic architecture, most farmsteads in the study area remained traditional in character. Conversely, consumerism and the acquisition of new products and household conveniences were evenly distributed among all study households.

Ironically, although modernization theory is a productive vehicle for potentially identifying the extent of material restructuring that occurred in rural contexts during the recent past, this strand of thought, when uncritically projected upon all rural situations in a large geographic and culturally heterogeneous region like the South, potentially serves to reify and exaggerate the beneficial impact of technological development and progress. The uncritical, qualitative use of modernization theory likewise obscures the actual material disparities and economic asymmetry that had persisted since Reconstruction in the South. From this perspective, modernization did indeed exert a significant influence upon rural life, but it was an influence that only initially benefited or was enjoyed by an affluent, minority segment of the population. This small proportion of the population possessed the necessary capital to establish modern farm operations and build modern dwellings. In contrast, the majority of rural residents during the middle of the twentieth century in the study area endured life experiences not far removed from those of their parents and grandparents. Significant economic and material change did not occur in the middle Savannah River valley until the second half of the twentieth century.

The trajectory of rural life in the study area during the middle of the twentieth century effectively illustrates that modernization, when present, can be readily identified through material culture. Material traits such as new dwelling styles, new dwelling construction materials, farm machinery, electrical hardware, canning jar glass, metal food containers, and items related to leisure time activities such as radio parts and phonograph record fragments all indicate that subtle but profound culture change was occurring in rural households from the late 1800s to the middle of the twentieth century.

Likewise, the degree of restructuring that occurred in a specific study area owing to modernization can also often be minimal. During the postbellum period, rural modernization was not occurring in the middle Savannah River valley. The lack of modernization in the study areas is perhaps best explained through political economy that recognizes the existence of internal, underdeveloped peripheries in North America and other developed core nations (Dunaway 1996). From this perspective, the absence of economic development in the study area and the lack of prosperity among most of the residents were probably due to numerous factors. The debilitating influence of cotton cultivation and the tenancy system, the effect of an agriculturally marginal environment, coupled with continuous population growth, and a finite amount of farmland, all served in concert to perpetuate the hardscrabble character of rural life in the area for a century or more. Interestingly, substantial transformation that encouraged the eventual demise of rural tenancy and cotton culture did not occur until the second half of the twentieth century, largely through a sustained federal government presence

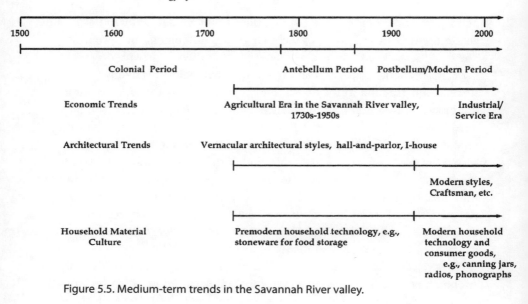

Figure 5.5. Medium-term trends in the Savannah River valley.

at the Savannah River Site and the establishment of manufacturing and industrial operations in the middle Savannah River valley.

Returning to the concepts of temporal theory and culture history introduced earlier, the medium-term history of the study area in this example is summarized in Figure 5.5. The importance of the recent historical past is clearly illustrated by the chart. As stated earlier, medium-term history in the middle Savannah River valley can be divided into the agricultural era, spanning an approximately 225-year interval, and the industrial/service era, comprising the past 50 years. Interestingly, although lesser currents of change were occurring during this period (such as progressive farming, consumerism, etc.), major structural change does not occur until the waning years of the agricultural era after World War II. The agricultural era is mainly characterized by economic, cultural, and material continuity, evident by the dogged persistence of similar agricultural practices, architectural traditions, and household material culture. Corresponding to the end of this agricultural era, after the 1950s the rural landscape began to change: New dwelling styles were adopted by larger segments of the population, and practically everyone became dependent upon consumer goods. Consequently, by focusing only on earlier archaeological resources and ignoring sites inhabited since the late nineteenth century, this important transition in rural material life would be overlooked. Further, the transition from an agricultural- to a postagricultural-based economy occurred throughout different farming areas of the United States at different times. The challenge for contemporary and future historical archaeologists is to understand more fully this recent but important transition within the culture history of rural America.

A Progressive Farmwife: Postbellum Life at the Drake Site

Frontier conditions prevailed in much of the Midwest during the first half of the 1800s. During the initial period of settlement between the late 1700s and the 1850s, pioneers from the Northeast, upper Southeast, and Europe established mixed farming in the region. Grain and livestock agriculture was a central component of frontier farming transplanted to the area by settler households. By the 1860s, corn and livestock farming developed into a substantial part of the region's agricultural economy. In turn, regional centers like Chicago, connected to the farming hinterlands by efficient railroad systems, became redistribution points for farm products raised in the Midwest.

During the second half of the 1800s, the Midwest became the breadbasket of the United States, encouraged by deep, fertile glacial soils and new farming and transportation technology. Midwest farmers during the postbellum period became increasingly concerned with progressive farming, involving the adoption of new farm technology and labor-saving devices within the home (McClelland 1997). At the same time during the second half of the 1800s, women began asserting their influence at home and publicly through the temperance and suffrage movements. Archaeology conducted at the Drake farmstead located in northwest Illinois illustrates material trends associated with a prosperous, progressive farmstead during the second half of the 1800s. This farmstead also illustrates how farm women began to exercise their independence during the late Victorian period in the Midwest.

The Drake farmstead site was located in northwest Illinois in Stephenson County (Figure 1.2). The site was investigated between 1983 and 1985 by archaeologists with Illinois State University (Phillippe 1990) as part of highway improvements associated with the Freeport Bypass Highway development project. Initially discovered during reconnaissance survey in 1983, the site was subsequently the subject of archaeological test excavations. Following site testing, the Drake farmstead was judged to be archaeologically significant and data-recovery excavations were conducted there in 1985. The site is important because it is one of the first farmsteads intensively studied through archaeology in northwest Illinois. The farmstead illustrates important material trends related to the standard of living and consumerism practiced among progressive Midwest farmers between the late antebellum and postbellum periods. The site also illustrates the influence that progressive-minded farm wives exercised in their households.

The Drake farmstead was located in Silver Creek Township near the town of Freeport, Illinois. Silver Creek Township was settled in 1835 by Thomas Craine. In 1836, other settlers arrived at Silver Creek, including Sidney Joel Stebbins from New York State. His first cousin, Chauncey Stebbins, joined Joel in 1838 and established a residence. Chauncey entered a land claim on June 22, 1842, and on May 1, 1843, purchased from the government the land tract that comprised his farmstead. Chauncey married Roxanna Minerva Stebbins, his cousin, in 1840, and they had four children. In September 1857, Chauncey and his daughter Mary became ill and died. Roxanna later remarried, to Lloyd Drake, in 1859. Lloyd died in 1896, and Roxanna a few years later in 1900. The farm was deeded to Amy Freeman, Roxanna's daughter, in 1896. The farm then passed from Homer Stebbins (a cousin) to Samuel Schmitt in 1900. By 1913 the property was abandoned and the structures at the farmstead were destroyed.

Between the 1830s and 1890s, the Drake site was a prosperous middle-class farm. Livestock and grain were the main products raised. In 1848, Chauncey and Roxanna Stebbins owned 452 acres, exceeding the county, state, and regional farm averages by two to three times. Likewise, they owned 200 head of cattle in 1857, the year Chauncey died, and the amount of livestock the Stebbinses owned was four times greater than the county, state, and regional averages enumerated in the 1860 federal census of agriculture. Corn and other grains were also raised at the farm, as indicated by a corn plow, corn sheller, fanning mill, harrows, reapers, and threshing machine listed in Chauncey's probate inventory. Chauncey and Roxanna owned three other farms that were operated by tenants, and they also received rent from a house they owned in the neighboring town of Freeport.

In addition to helping operate a successful farm, Roxanna Drake was a socially progressive individual, as illustrated by several surviving historical records associated with her life. When Chauncey Stebbins died in 1857, Roxanna contested the first probate inventory and requested that a second inventory be conducted. She probably made this request because her husband was a wealthy man and she was not satisfied with the amount of his estate that she was to receive, as stipulated by inheritance law. Consequently, she probably requested a larger share of the widow's dower. In addition to carefully managing her financial matters, Roxanna also subscribed to *The New Covenant*, a progressive newspaper that supported the temperance movement, women's suffrage, and the abolition of slavery. After her first husband died in 1857, she married Lloyd Drake. In 1871, she further asserted her independence when she had a lithograph illustration made of her farmhouse. The lithograph's caption states: "Res. Of Roxanna Drake, Sec. 2 Silver Creek TP. Stephenson Co. Ill." It is noteworthy that the dwelling is described as the residence of Roxanna Drake. Lloyd, her husband, is not mentioned. Likewise, Lloyd and Roxanna were also listed in the *History of Stephenson County*, which states that: "LLOYD DRAKE farmer, Sec. 2: P.O. Freeport born Dec. 19, 1818 in Tioga Co., N.Y. In 1857, he came to Belvidere, Ill., [In] April, 1859, he removed to Stephenson Co.; Mrs. Drake owns 186 acres of land. He married Mrs. Stebbins in 1859. She was born in Madison Co., N.Y. April 10, 1819; came to Stephenson Co. in 1840; she has three children by a former marriage—Charles J., Amy now Mrs. Freeman, and Frances R. now Mrs. Shirk" (*History of Stephenson County* 1880: 679). Apparently, Roxanna felt compelled to have her land listed separately from her husband Lloyd, as illustrated in the quote.

During data-recovery excavations at the Drake farmstead, six features were encountered, consisting of the dwelling's stone-lined cellar (measuring ca. 16 by 24 by 4 feet), a foundation segment associated with a later addition to the farmhouse, a cellar associated with the later addition, a well, a cistern, and a privy vault (Figure 5.6). Extant historical information and the archaeological data recovered from site excavations indicate three main occupational events occurred at the farmstead. In 1838, when the site was first occupied, Chauncey Stebbins constructed the dwelling that stood over the 16-by-24-foot stone-lined cellar. This original dwelling was probably similar to a story-and-a-half New England wooden frame cottage. The well and cistern were also constructed at this time. In 1850, the cellar entryway and cistern were partially filled to allow construction of a second cellar and a frame addition to the dwelling. Half a century later, between 1896 and 1900, the farm was abandoned. At this time the structures at the farm were razed, the cellars beneath the dwelling were filled, and the well and privy at the farm were also filled. The features encountered during excavations revealed the site structure of the farmstead and also produced a large number of artifacts relevant to understanding daily material conditions at the Drake farmstead.

Regarding the arrangement of the farm lot, surviving historical records and archaeological information indicate that by 1871 the Drake farm en-

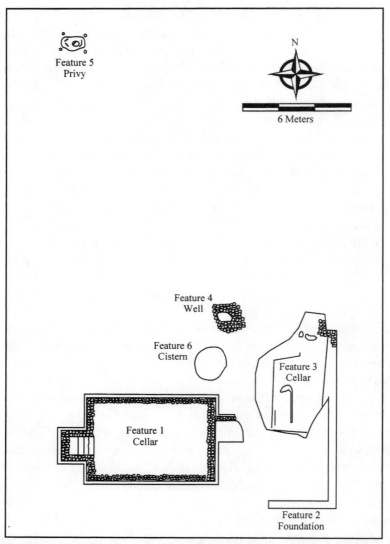

Figure 5.6. Map of the house lot at the Drake farm. By permission of Illinois State University, from Phillippe 1990, Figure 13, p. 37.

compassed the southeast quarter of Section 2 in Stephenson County. The dwelling was located in the southeast corner of the tract, and a barn was located west of the house lot. The house lot was surrounded by an iron fence, and the dwelling depicted in the 1871 lithograph appears to be similar to a two-story I-house with an ell located in the rear of the dwelling. The ell was probably the original dwelling constructed in the 1830s that corresponds

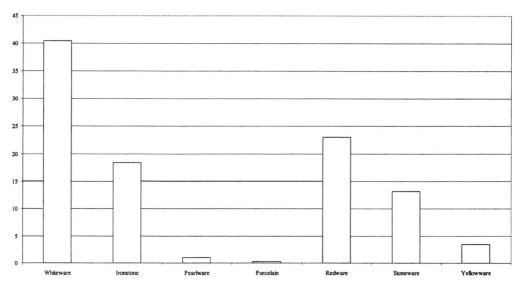

Figure 5.7. Distribution of ceramics by ware recovered from the Drake farm.

to the earlier 16-by-24-foot stone-lined cellar encountered during excavations.

Artifacts recovered from excavation provide important information about daily life at the farm, especially foodways and health care practiced by the site residents. Faunal material recovered from the Drake farm indicates that pork was the meat of choice among the site residents, followed by a smaller proportion of beef. The site residents did not consume any wild game. Although the residents of the Drake farm were prosperous, the ceramics recovered from the site suggest that Roxanna Drake was frugal regarding ceramic purchasing decisions. Whiteware (40.48 percent, n=1055) and ironstone (18.45 percent, n=481) ceramics were the predominant tableware. Porcelain (0.3 percent, n=8) and pearlware (0.99 percent, n=26) were minority table ceramics and were underrepresented in the assemblage. Utilitarian food storage, processing, and consumption ceramics are represented by redware (23.06 percent, n=601), stoneware (13.16 percent, n=343), and yellowware (3.53 percent, n=92) (Figure 5.7). Considered by decoration, painted wares (including annular, edge-decorated, hand-painted, and sponged techniques) comprise 63 percent (n=392) of the decorated tableware followed by transfer-printed (18 percent, n=115), luster (11 percent, n=67), and moulded ceramics (8 percent, n=51). Based on the variety of ceramics recovered from the farm, Roxanna Drake chose moderately priced painted whiteware and ironstone as the primary tableware used in her residence. Interestingly, porcelain, an expensive ceramic, is practically nonexistent in the assemblage. Likewise, costlier transfer-printed ceramics comprise less than a quarter of the tableware sample, suggesting transfer-printed vessels were used, but to a lesser extent than moderate-priced painted tableware.

In addition to the foodways artifacts recovered from the farm, a large collection of glass containers was recovered from excavations. Based upon a minimum glass vessel count, a total of 1,267 glass containers were functionally identified. The functional distribution of the identified glass containers is presented in Table 5.2. Over a quarter (28 percent) of the identified glass containers were medicine bottles. These items reveal important details about the health care practices used by the site residents. A total of 363 glass medicine containers were identified in the minimum vessel count. Of these 363 containers, one-third (n=119) were from patent or proprietary medicines. Patent medicines were popular during the second half of the nineteenth century. They were intended to cure a broad range of health problems. Many of them contained large amounts of alcohol and narcotics, such as opium and cocaine. The dubious benefits of patent medicines became widely known among physicians by the late 1800s, and they became illegal with the passage of the U.S. Food and Drug Act in 1906. The patent medicine bottle fragments recovered from the Drake farm were embossed with the product's name, allowing the identification of the container's contents. The remaining two-thirds of the medicine bottle containers in the minimum vessel count were prescription medicine containers, indicating their contents had been prescribed by a doctor and the bottles filled at a pharmacy.

During the final third of the site's occupation, the residents of the Drake farm spent several hundred dollars on patent medicines and used over 30 different brands. Interestingly, Roxanna Drake was socially progressive and subscribed to newspapers that espoused the temperance movement. Likewise, alcohol containers comprised less than 6 percent of the total glass bottle sample, indicating the farm residents were probably teetotalers and did not frequently drink alcohol. Consequently, it seems likely that the farm residents were sincere and legitimately used the patent medicines for health purposes. Admittedly, the farm residents may not have been fully aware of the alcoholic and narcotic contents or effects of the medicines; otherwise they probably would not have used them, given the fact that they appeared to have been teetotalers. The range of patent medicines recovered from the

Table 5.2. Functional Distribution of Glass Bottle Fragments Recovered from the Drake Farm

Function	Number	Percentage
Alcoholic beverages	74	5.84
Non-alcoholic beverages	26	2.05
Commercial food	13	1.03
Home canning	791	62.43
Medicine	363	28.65
Total	1,267	100.00

Source: Phillippe 1990: 162.

site indicates that the medicines were being used to relieve four main health problems among the residents: bone and joint ailments, digestive disorders, respiratory problems, and female complaints.

The Drake farmstead illustrates the complex character of rural life in the Midwest during the second half of the 1800s. The residents of the farm owned a large amount of land and livestock compared to their neighbors, in addition to several tenant farms. A commercially oriented, progressive approach to farming can be surmised by the extent of the agricultural operations maintained by the site's residents and the farm machines listed in the probate inventory. Roxanna Drake, the matriarch of the family, was also apparently an independently oriented person who kept a careful eye on her finances. In contrast to Victorian period stereotypes emphasizing that women were to be cloistered in the home and passively obey their husbands, Roxanna appears to have valued her personal autonomy.

Materially, rural socioeconomic class was probably conveyed by the residents through the farm itself, including land, improvements, and the dwelling. In contrast, Roxanna Drake chose not to make frequent expensive ceramic purchases but mainly used moderately priced painted tableware. Interestingly, however, practical health concerns were important to the household members, and the residents expended a noticeable amount of money on medicine, illustrated archaeologically by the quantity of medicine container glass recovered from excavations. Further, the range of medicine brands recovered from the Drake farm indicates that during the second half of the 1800s, the residents had unimpeded access to consumer goods originating throughout North America. The consumer behavior of the farm residents also highlights the fact that historical archaeologists should be cautious in their material expectations of rural households: Expensive ceramics were not a priority to most families, and, given the choice, household finances even among affluent farmers were often expended on more practical, immediate needs, such as medicine, as opposed to nonutilitarian furnishings like expensive tableware.

6

Future Directions in the Archaeology of Farmsteads

Constructing Regional Models of Rural Material Life

As illustrated by the case studies discussed in the preceding chapters, in many respects farmsteads are similar to the domestic sites typically investigated by archaeologists. Consequently, similar archaeological questions prevalent in domestic sites archaeology are usually addressed during the excavation of farm residences: How long did the residents live at a site? What kind of dwelling did they live in? What type and quality of food did they eat? What types of household items did they use—homemade or locally made objects, such as redware or stoneware pottery, or factory-produced goods? To what extent were the site's residents and social relations influenced by national trends, such as industrialization, modernization, immigration, and popular culture?

Beyond these basic interpretive questions that are usually addressed at most domestic sites, farmsteads are relatively different from typical non-farming domestic sites. Farmsteads were self-contained, household-level, production-consumption units, meaning foodstuffs were raised on the farm, consumed by the farm household, and also marketed for profit. The basic economic activities conducted at a farm in turn could potentially influence daily material life in important ways, such as the arrangement of the farm and house lot, the function and placement of outbuildings, the types of food consumed by the household, gender roles in the household, and the standard of living experienced by the site's residents.

In addition to site-specific economic activities, farmsteads often possess time depth and household/cultural continuity not usually encountered at the average domestic site. At many farmsteads, sons, daughters, grandchildren, and great-grandchildren inherited and worked the land at the family home place, often for a century or more. Consequently, farmsteads offer many intriguing interpretive opportunities and challenges that are unique to this site type. For example, at farms with appreciable time depth occupied by the same lineal or extended family, archaeologists can potentially track material changes influenced by socioeconomic class, ethnicity, race, gender, or religious affiliation. As illustrated by the preceding examples, the archaeological study of farmsteads is limited only by our imagination, creativity, and the questions that we ask of the material record.

From a pragmatic point of view, one potentially productive way of studying farmsteads in the future is to approach them from a perspective emphasizing multiple scales of analysis (Orser 1996: 186–188). Not unlike the zoom function on a computer-mapping program, archaeologists should couch their questions in terms of global, national, regional, community, site, and household contexts. By creating interplay between these different spatial scales, enhanced understanding of material life at farmsteads can be achieved. For example, cultural geographers interested in the topic of agricultural geography (e.g., Anderson 1973; Tarrant 1974; Symons 1979) emphasize that the distinctive characteristics of rural material life in the various regions of North America are significantly influenced by regionally specific environments, crop regimes, and agricultural economies. Some historical archaeologists, especially those who study the archaeology of plantations, have likewise acknowledged the important influence of different crop regimes upon production strategies, plantation spatial organization, and social relations (e.g., Orser 1988a). In contrast, historical archaeologists studying farmsteads have not yet collectively articulated a set of central, organizing goals or an explicitly formulated research design broadly applicable to a wide range of historical situations and rural production types in North America.

Consequently, it is proposed that individuals interested in exploring the medium-duration temporal processes associated with farmstead archaeology should attempt to construct regionally based models that examine the interrelated topics of agricultural production types and material life within specific physiographic zones (Groover 1998). A few studies have applied this method with promising results. As discussed, in the study of farms near Aiken, South Carolina (Cabak and Inkrot 1997; Cabak et al. 1999), a large sample of operator and tenant farmsteads inhabited between 1875 and 1950 was examined using the concept of modernization as a theoretical interpretive theme. Interestingly, by looking at domestic architecture preserved within archival records and household material culture recovered archaeologically, it was determined that rural architecture lagged considerably in the realm of modernization, whereas most people were using modern consumer products and household items by the early twentieth century. The surprising endurance of rural architectural forms into the middle twentieth century that first appeared during the colonial and antebellum periods in the study area was attributed to the debilitating effects of the tenant system and cotton cultivation upon the rural population. These findings were unexpected and seriously question broad generalizations concerning the beneficial and transformative effects that modernization exerted upon the rural landscape of the Lower South that have been advanced by historical studies of twentieth-century rural life.

Beyond a regional approach, by focusing upon the topics of agricultural production, land- and wealth-holding trends, inheritance customs, domestic architecture, and consumerism, the economic, cultural, and material trends present at household and community levels in rural settings can be reconstructed. This exercise can provide a powerful interpretive context and a useful research framework. To fully implement this proposed research strategy, the rural economic groups or class structure defined through land and tax records and farming production records can be systematically sampled through the archaeological record, to define the material variation that existed between different socioeconomic groups or classes. Further, an important goal of future inquiry would be to define how wealth differences translate to the archaeological record and the built environment. This task could be accomplished by systematically investigating sites associated with firmly documented households from different socioeconomic groups within tax districts and counties, based on land, tax, and probate records. An effort of this extent, which has yet to be fully attempted in historical archaeology, would eventually result in an archaeological database composed of cases representing all economic segments of a past rural population for a defined interval of time within a study area. The material differences and similarities that existed among different population segments, socioeconomic classes, ethnic groups, racial groups, and religious denominations could then be defined with a reliable level of quantitative precision.

In summary, this research strategy, directed at reconstructing quantitatively based regional models of agricultural production and material life, could be used in practically any geographic context in North America. The main steps in replicating the research strategy in different areas involve first reconstructing medium-duration temporal processes within the previously discussed domains of rural economy and material life that are characteristic of a specific region, then intensively examining the particulars represented by sites, or individual case studies. At the intraregional level, the long-term information return from this endeavor would certainly justify the initial effort required in constructing an interpretive model of this extent.

After the initial implementation of the proposed research strategy, newly discovered or excavated archaeological sites could be placed or contextually grounded within the model through consideration of the previously discussed analysis variables. Moreover, an effort of this scope, conducted in concert by several researchers located in different geographic regions, such as the Northeast, the Mid-Atlantic, the Southeast, the Midwest, and the trans-Mississippi West, could potentially result in a national-level synthesis of rural economy and material life in North America based on analysis of specific production types and material characteristics associated with different regions.

This research strategy may at first sound incredibly unrealistic. However, in many states the basic pieces of the archaeological puzzle—previously recorded farm sites—already exist in abundance. In turn, two primary steps are needed to develop regionally based research strategies for farmstead archaeology: the creation of historic contexts for farm sites in different areas of the United States and placing existing farm sites within this interpretive context. Fortunately, many states already have historic context documents and preservation plans that address relevant research themes for rural sites (such as Delaware, Louisiana, and Georgia, to name a few), but many, unfortunately, have yet to develop these archaeological management research documents. If extant archaeological information is assembled, then syntheses of farmstead archaeology could be periodically produced for different regions in North America.

The responsibility of developing research strategies for archaeological resources related to rural life should not be entirely shouldered by state or federal historic preservation agencies, however. State-supported and private universities with historical archaeology research specializations, federally managed land reserves, and state-maintained landholdings, such as parks and forests, could all potentially benefit and contribute to the archaeological study of farmsteads. In reality, over the long term, farmstead sites will continue to be encountered during cultural management studies in the United States, and, as time passes, their age will only increase, further contributing to their validity as important archaeological resources that must be effectively managed, preserved, and studied.

References Cited

Adams, Jane. 1993. Resistance to "Modernity": Southern Illinois Farm Women and the Cult of Domesticity. *American Ethnologist* 20(1): 89–113.

Adams, William H. (editor). 1980. *Waverly Plantation: Ethnoarchaeology of a Tenant Farming Community*. National Technical Information Service, Washington, D.C.

———. 1990. Landscape Archaeology, Landscape History, and the American Farmstead. *Historical Archaeology* 24(4): 92–101.

Adams, William H., and Sarah J. Boling. 1989. Status and Ceramics for Planters and Slaves on Three Georgia Coastal Plantations. *Historical Archaeology* 23(1): 69–96.

Ahlman, Todd. 1996. Backwards Farmers or Modernizing Farms? The Tennessee Valley Farms of East Tennessee in the Early Twentieth Century. Unpublished Master's thesis, Department of Anthropology, University of Tennessee, Knoxville.

Alston, Lee J., and Joseph P. Ferrie. 2005. Time on the Ladder: Career Mobility in Agriculture, 1890–1938. *The Journal of Economic History* 65: 1058–1081.

Anderson, James R. 1973. *A Geography of Agriculture in the United States' Southeast*. Akadémiai Kiadó, Budapest, Hungary.

Appleby, Joyce O. 1982. Commercial Farming and the Agrarian Myth in the Early Republic. *Journal of American History* 68: 833–849.

Ascher, Robert, and Charles H. Fairbanks. 1971. Excavation of a Slave Cabin: Georgia, U.S.A. *Historical Archaeology* 5: 3–17.

Ayers, Edward L. 1992. *The Promise of the New South: Life After Reconstruction*. Oxford University Press, Oxford, England.

Babson, David W. 1990. The Archaeology of Racism and Ethnicity on Southern Plantations. *Historical Archaeology* 24(4): 20–28.

Baugher, Sherene, and Terry H. Klein. 2003. Historic Preservation and the Archaeology of Nineteenth-Century Farmsteads in the Northeast. Special issue of *Northeast Historical Archaeology*, vols. 30–31 (2001–2002).

Baumann, Timothy E. 2001. "Because That's Where My Roots Are": Searching for Patterns of African-American Ethnicity in Arrow Rock, Missouri. Unpublished Ph.D. dissertation, Department of Anthropology, University of Tennessee, Knoxville.

Bedell, John, Michael Petraglia, and Thomas Plummer. 1994. Status, Technology, and Rural Tradition in Western Pennsylvania: Excavations at the Shaeffer Farm Site. *Northeast Historical Archaeology* 23: 29–58.

Bedell, John, Michael Petraglia, Dennis Knepper, and Thomas Plummer. 1993. Excavations at 36AR410, a Nineteenth-Century Rural Domestic Residence in Armstrong County, Pennsylvania. Ms. on file, Bureau for Historic Preservation, Harrisburg, Pennsylvania.

Beedle, Peggy Lee. 1996. *The Farm Landscape*. State Historical Society of Wisconsin, Madison.

Braudel, Fernand. 1971. *The Mediterranean and the Mediterranean World in the Age of Phillip II*. Collins, London.

———. 1974. *Capitalism and Material Life, 1400–1800*. Harper and Row, New York.

———. 1977. *Afterthoughts on Material Civilization and Capitalism*. John Hopkins University Press, Baltimore, Maryland.

———. 1980. *On History*. University of Chicago Press, Chicago, Illinois.

———. 1981. *The Structures of Everyday Life: The Limits of the Possible*. Harper and Row, New York.

Brooks, Richard D. 1987. *250 Years of Historic Occupation on Steel Creek, Savannah River Plant, Barnwell County, South Carolina*. Savannah River Archaeological Research Program, South Carolina Institute of Archaeology and Anthropology, University of South Carolina, Columbia.

Brooks, Richard D., Mark D. Groover, and Samuel C. Smith. 2000. *Living on the Edge: The Archaeology of Cattle Raisers in the South Carolina Backcountry*. Savannah River Archaeological Research Papers 10. Savannah River Archaeological Research Program, South Carolina Institute of Archaeology and Anthropology, University of South Carolina, Columbia.

Brown, Ethel Gibbs. 1987. Interview with Mrs. Ethel Gibbs Brown. Cassette tape on file, Department of Anthropology, University of Tennessee, Knoxville.

Brown, Margaret Kimball, and Lawrie Cena Dean. 1995. *The French Colony in the Mid-Mississippi Valley*. American Kestrel Books, Carbondale, Illinois.

Cabak, Melanie A., and Mark D. Groover. 2004. *Plantations Without Pillars: Archaeology, Wealth, and Material Life at Bush Hill*, Volume 1: *Context and Interpretation*. Savannah River Archaeological Research Papers 11. Savannah River Archaeological Research Program, South Carolina Institute of Archaeology and Anthropology, University of South Carolina, Columbia.

———. 2006. Bush Hill: Material Life at a Working Plantation. *Historical Archaeology* 40(4): 51–83.

Cabak, Melanie A., and Mary M. Inkrot. 1997. *Old Farm, New Farm: An Archaeology of Rural Modernization in the Aiken Plateau, 1875–1950*. Savannah River Archaeological Research Papers 9. Occasional Papers of the Savannah River Archaeological Research Program, South Carolina Institute of Archaeology and Anthropology, University of South Carolina, Columbia.

Cabak, Melanie A., and Amy L. Young. 1998. Engendering African-American Archaeology. Organized session presented at the 31st Annual Meeting of the Society for Historical Archaeology Conference on Historical and Underwater Archaeology, Atlanta, Georgia.

Cabak, Melanie A., Mark D. Groover, and Mary M. Inkrot. 1999. Rural Modernization During the Recent Past: Farmstead Archaeology in the Aiken Plateau. *Historical Archaeology* 33(4): 19–43.

Cabak, Melanie A., Mark D. Groover, and Scott J. Wagers. 1995. Health Care and the Wayman A.M.E. Church. *Historical Archaeology* 29(2): 55–76.

Carson, Cary, Norman F. Barka, William M. Kelso, Gary Wheeler Stone, and Dell Upton. 1988. Impermanent Architecture in the Southern American Colonies. In *Material Life in America: 1600–1860*, edited by Robert Blair St. George, pp. 113–158. Northeastern University Press, Boston.

Catts, Wade P., Jay F. Custer, JoAnn E. Jamison, Michael D. Scholl, and Karen Iplenski. 1995. *Final Archaeological Investigations at the Strickland Plantation Site (7K-AK-117), A Mid-Eighteenth Century Farmstead, State Route 1 Corridor, Smyrna, Kent County, Delaware*. Delaware Department of Transportation Archaeology Series No. 119. Prepared by the University of Delaware Center for Archaeological Research, Newark.

Cheek, Charles D., and Amy Friedlander. 1990. Pottery and Pig's Feet: Space, Ethnicity, and Neighborhood in Washington, D.C., 1880–1940. *Historical Archaeology* 24(1): 34–60.

Clarke, David V. 2001. Defining and Integrating Sequences in Site Analysis: The Evidence from Hillforts and Other Sites. *Oxford Journal of Archaeology* 20(3): 293–306.

Crass, David C., and Mark J. Brooks. 1995. *Cotton and Black Draught: Consumer Behavior on a Postbellum Farm*. Savannah River Archaeological Research Papers 5. Savannah River Archaeologial Research Program, South Carolina Institute of Archaeology and Anthropology, University of South Carolina, Columbia.

Deagan, Kathleen. 1982. Avenues of Inquiry in Historical Archaeology. In *Advances in Archaeological Method and Theory*, Vol. 5, pp. 151–177. Academic Press, New York.

De Cunzo, Lu Ann. 2004. *A Historical Archaeology of Delaware: People, Contexts, and the Cultures of Agriculture*. University of Tennessee Press, Knoxville.

De Cunzo, Lu Ann, and Wade P. Catts. 1990. *Management Plan for Delaware's Historical Archaeological Resources*. University of Delaware Center for Archaeological Research, Newark.

Deetz, James. 1977. *In Small Things Forgotten: The Archaeology of Early American Life*. Doubleday, New York.

Denker, Bert R. (editor). 1996. *The Substance of Style: Perspectives on the American Arts and Crafts Movement*. University Press of New England, Hanover, New Hampshire.

Dunaway, Wilma A. 1996. *The First American Frontier: Transition to Capitalism in Southern Appalachia, 1700–1860*. University of North Carolina Press, Chapel Hill.

Fairbanks, Charles H. 1972. The Kingsley Slave Cabins in Duval County, Florida, 1968. *Conference on Historic Site Archaeology Papers, 1971* 7: 62–93.

———. 1984. The Plantation Archaeology of the Southeastern Coast. *Historical Archaeology* 18(1): 1–14.

Faulkner, Charles H. 1988a. *Archaeological Testing at the Nicholas Gibbs House: Season I*. Prepared for the Nicholas Gibbs Historical Society by the Department of Anthropology, University of Tennessee, Knoxville.

———. 1988b. The Gibbs House: Excavation of a Late 18th Century German-American Farmstead in Knox County, Tennessee. *Ohio Valley Historical Archaeology* 6: 1–8.

———. 1989. *Archaeological Testing at the Nicholas Gibbs House: Season II*. Prepared for the Nicholas Gibbs Historical Society by the Department of Anthropology, University of Tennessee, Knoxville.

———. 1991. *Archaeological Testing at the Nicholas Gibbs House: Season III*. Prepared for the Nicholas Gibbs Historical Society by the Department of Anthropology, University of Tennessee, Knoxville.

———. 1992. An Archaeological Study of Fences at the Gibbs House. *Proceedings of the Tenth Symposium on Ohio Valley Urban and Historic Archaeology*, pp. 31–41. Miscellaneous Paper No. 16, Tennessee Anthropological Association, Knoxville.

———. 1998. "Here are Frame Houses and Brick Chimneys": Knoxville, Tennessee in the Late Eighteenth Century. In *The Southern Colonial Backcountry: Interdisciplinary Perspectives on Frontier Communities*, edited by D. C. Crass, S. D. Smith, M. A. Zierden, and R. D. Brooks, pp. 137–161. University of Tennessee Press, Knoxville.

Feder, Kenneth L. 2007. *The Past in Perspective: An Introduction to Human Prehistory*. McGraw Hill, New York.

Ferguson, Leland. 1992. *Uncommon Ground: Archaeology and Early African America, 1650–1800*. Smithsonian Institution Press, Washington, D.C.

Fite, Gilbert C. 1981. *American Farmers: The New Minority*. Indiana University Press, Bloomington.

———. 1984. *Cotton Fields No More: Southern Agriculture, 1865–1980*. University Press of Kentucky, Lexington.

Forehand, Tammy R., Mark D. Groover, David C. Crass, and Robert Moon. 2004. Bridging the Gap Between Archaeologists and the Public: Excavations at Silver Bluff Plantation, the George Galphin Site. *Early Georgia* 32(1): 51–73.

Forman, Henry C. 1948. *The Architecture of the Old South: The Medieval Style, 1585–1850*. Russell and Russell, New York.

Friedberger, Mark. 1988. *Farm Families and Change in Twentieth-Century America*. University Press of Kentucky, Lexington.

Friedlander, Amy. 1991. House and Barn: The Wealth of Farmers, 1795–1815. *Historical Archaeology* 25(2): 15–30.

Galle, Jillian, and Amy L. Young. 2004. *Engendering African-American Archaeology: A Southern Perspective*. University of Tennessee Press, Knoxville.

Glickman, Lawrence (editor). 1999. *Consumer Society in American History: A Reader*. Cornell University Press, Ithaca, New York.

Goody, Jack. 1978. *The Developmental Cycle in Domestic Groups*. Cambridge University Press, New York.

Grettler, D. J., D. C. Bachman, J. F. Custer, and J. Jamison. 1991. *Phase II Archaeological Survey of All Historic Sites in the Early Action Segment of the State Route 1 Relief Route, Delaware*. Delaware Department of Transportation Archaeology Series No. 87. Prepared by the University of Delaware Center for Archaeological Research, Newark.

Groover, Mark D. 1991. Of Mindset and Material Culture: An Archaeological View of Continuity and Change in the 18th-Century South Carolina Backcountry. Unpublished Master's thesis, Department of Anthropology, University of South Carolina, Columbia.

———. 1992a. *Of Mindset and Material Culture: An Archaeological View of Continuity and Change in the 18th-Century South Carolina Backcountry*. Volumes in Historical Archaeology XX. Conference on Historic Site Archaeology, University of South Carolina, Columbia.

———. 1992b. *Illinois Farmstead Archaeology: Past Issues, Future Goals*. Report submitted to Illinois Department of Transportation, Springfield. Prepared by Midwestern Archaeological Research Center, Illinois State University, Normal.

———. 1993. The Upland South Tradition as an Archaeological Model: A Comparison of Sites in Illinois, Tennessee, and South Carolina. *Ohio Valley Historical Archaeology* 10: 7–16.

———. 1994. Evidence for Folkways and Cultural Exchange in the 18th-Century South Carolina Backcountry. *Historical Archaeology* 28(1): 41–64.

———. 1998. The Gibbs Farmstead: An Archaeological Study of Rural Economy and Material Life in Southern Appalachia, 1790–1920. Ph.D. dissertation, Department of Anthropology, University of Tennessee, Knoxville. University Microfilms International, Ann Arbor, Michigan.

———. 2000. Creolization and the Archaeology of Multiethnic Households in the American South. *Historical Archaeology* 34(3): 99–106.

———. 2001. Linking Artifact Assemblages to Household Cycles: An Example from the Gibbs Site. *Historical Archaeology* 35(4): 38–57.

———. 2003. *An Archaeological Study of Rural Capitalism and Material Life: The Gibbs Farmstead in Southern Appalachia*. Springer, New York.

———. 2004. Household Succession as a Catalyst of Landscape Change. *Historical Archaeology* 38(4): 25–42.

———. 2005. The Gibbs Farmstead: Household Archaeology in an Internal Periphery. *International Journal of Historical Archaeology* 9(4): 229–289.

Groover, Mark D., and Richard D. Brooks. 2003. The Catherine Brown Cowpen and Thomas Howell Site: Material Characteristics of Cattle Raisers in the South Carolina Backcountry. *Southeastern Archaeology* 22(1): 92–111.

Gums, Bonnie L., William R. Iseminger, Molly E. McKenzie, and Dennis D. Nichols. 1991. The French Colonial Villages of Cahokia and Prairie du Pont, Illinois. In *French Colonial Archaeology: The Illinois Country and the Western Great Lakes*, edited by John A. Walthall, pp. 85–122. University of Illinois Press, Urbana.

Hardesty, Donald L. 1980. Historic Sites Archaeology on the Western American Frontier: Theoretical Perspectives and Research Problems. *North American Archaeologist* 2(1): 67–81.

Hardesty, Donald L., and Barbara J. Little. 2000. *Assessing Site Significance: A Guide for Archaeologists and Historians*. Altamira Press, New York.

Hart, John P., and Charles L. Fisher. 2000. *Nineteenth- and Early Twentieth-Century Domestic Site Archaeology in New York State*. New York State Museum Bulletin 495. University of the State of New York and the State Education Department, Albany.

Haviland, William A. 1994. *Anthropology*. 7th edition. Harcourt Brace College Publishers, New York.

Hillier, Bevis, and Stephen Escritt. 1997. *Art Deco Style*. Phaidon, London, England.

History of Stephenson County, Illinois. 1880. Western Historical Company, Chicago.

Horn, James P. 1988. "The Bare Necessities": Standards of Living in England and the Chesapeake, 1650–1700. *Historical Archaeology* 22(2): 74–91.

Jakle, John A., Robert W. Bastian, and Douglas K. Meyer. 1989. *Common Houses in*

America's Small Towns: The Atlantic Seaboard to the Mississippi Valley. University of Georgia Press, Athens.

Jordan, Terry G., and Matti Kaups. 1989. *The American Backwoods Frontier: An Ethnic and Ecological Interpretation.* Johns Hopkins University Press, Baltimore.

Joseph, J. W., Mary B. Reed, and Charles E. Cantley. 1991. *Agrarian Life, Romantic Death: Archaeological and Historical Testing and Data Recovery for the I-85 Northern Alternative, Spartanburg County, South Carolina.* Technical Report 39. Submitted to South Carolina Department of Highways and Public Transportation, Columbia. Prepared by New South Associates, Stone Mountain, Georgia.

Jurney, David H., and Randall W. Moir (editors). 1987. *Historic Buildings, Material Culture, and People of the Prairie Margin: Architecture, Artifacts, and Synthesis of Historic Archaeology.* Richland Creek Technical Series, Volume V. Archaeology Research Program, Institute for the Study of Earth and Man. Southern Methodist University, Dallas, Texas.

Jurney, David H., Susan A. Lebo, and Melissa M. Green. 1988. *Historic Farming on the Hogwallow Prairies: Ethnoarchaeological Investigations of the Mountain Creek Area, North Central Texas.* Joe Pool Lake Archaeological Project, Volume II. Archaeological Research Program, Institute for the Study of Earth and Man, Southern Methodist University, Dallas, Texas.

Kelso, William M. 1984. *Kingsmill Plantations, 1619–1800: Archaeology of Country Life in Colonial Virginia.* Academic Press, New York.

Kelso, William H., and Rachel Most (editors). 1990. *Earth Patterns: Essays in Landscape Archaeology.* University Press of Virginia, Charlottesville.

King, Julia. 1994. Rural Landscape in the Mid-Nineteenth-Century Chesapeake. In *Historical Archaeology of the Chesapeake*, edited by Paul Shackel and Barbara Little, pp. 283–299. Smithsonian Institution Press, Washington, D.C.

Kleinegger, Christine. 2001. Out of the Barns and Into the Kitchens: Transformations in Farm Women's Work in the First Half of the Twentieth Century. In *American Technology (Blackwell Readers in American Social and Cultural History)*, edited by Carroll Pusell, pp. 169–207. Blackwell Publishers, Malden, Massachusetts.

Kovacik, Charles F., and John J. Winberry. 1987. *South Carolina: A Geography.* Westview Press, Boulder, Colorado.

Kulikoff, Allan. 1986. *Tobacco and Slaves: The Development of Southern Cultures in the Chesapeake, 1680–1800.* University of North Carolina Press, Chapel Hill.

———. 1992. *The Agrarian Origins of American Capitalism.* University Press of Virginia, Charlottesville.

Leone, Mark P. 2005. *The Archaeology of Liberty in an American Capital: Excavations in Annapolis.* University of California Press, Berkeley.

Leone, Mark P., and Gladys Marie-Fry. 1999. Conjuring in the Big House Kitchen: An Interpretation of African-American Belief Systems Based on the Uses of Archaeology and Folklore Sources. *Journal of American Folklore* 112(445): 372–403.

Leone, Mark P., Cheryl Janifer LaRoche, and Jennifer J. Babiarz. 2005. The Archaeology of Black Americans in Recent Times. *Annual Review of Anthropology* 34: 575–598.

Levendowski, J., and D. Loren. 1995. *Cultural Resource Management Survey, Paragraph*

3 *Reconnaissance Survey, PIN 9102.11/BIN 1–04230–0, Route 235 Over Wylie Brook, Town of Coventry, Chenango County.* Report prepared for the New York State Museum, State Education Department by Public Archaeology Facility, State University of New York at Binghamton, New York.

Levendowski, J., and N. Versaggi. 1995. *Site Examination, PIN 9102.11/BIN 1–04230–0, Route 235 Over Wylie Brook, Town of Coventry, Chenango County.* Report prepared for the New York State Museum, State Education Department by Public Archaeology Facility, State University of New York at Binghamton, New York.

Levy, Marion J., Jr. 1967. Social Patterns (Structures) and Problems of Modernization. In *Readings on Social Change*, edited by Wilbert Moore and Robert M. Cooks, pp. 189–208. Prentice-Hall, Englewood Cliffs, New Jersey.

Linebaugh, Donald W., and G. G. Robinson (editors). 1994. *Spatial Patterning in Historical Archaeology: Selected Studies of Settlement.* King and Queen Press, College of William and Mary, Williamsburg, Virginia.

Little, Barbara J. 1994. People with History: An Update on Historical Archaeology in the United States. *Journal of Archaeological Method and Theory* 1(1): 5–40.

Mascia, Sara F. 1994. Climbing the Agricultural Ladder: An Archaeological and Documentary Case Study of the Transition from Tenant to Owner on a New England Farmstead. Ph.D. dissertation, Department of Archaeology, Boston University. University Microfilms International, Ann Arbor, Michigan.

———. 1996. "One of the Best Farms in Essex County": The Changing Domestic Landscape of a Tenant Who Became an Owner. In *Landscape Archaeology: Reading and Interpreting the American Historical Landscape*, edited by Rebecca Yamin and Karen Bescherer Metheny, pp. 148–174. University of Tennessee Press, Knoxville.

Mathison, Marie. 1987. Outbuilding Locations on the Nicholas Gibbs House Site: A Preliminary Report. Manuscript on file, Department of Anthropology, University of Tennessee, Knoxville.

McAlester, Virginia, and Lee McAlester. 1984. *A Field Guide to American Houses.* Alfred A. Knopf, New York.

McClelland, Peter D. 1997. *Sowing Modernity: America's First Agricultural Revolution.* Cornell University Press, Ithaca, New York.

McCorvie, Mary R. 1987. *The Davis, Baldridge, and Huggins Sites: Three Nineteenth Century Upland South Farmsteads in Perry County, Illinois.* Preservation Series 4, American Resources Group, Ltd., Carbondale, Illinois.

McCorvie, Mary R., Mark J. Wagner, Jane K. Johnston, Terrance J. Martin, and Kathryn E. Parker. 1989. *Archaeological Investigations at the Fair View Farm Site: A Historic Farmstead in the Shawnee Hills of Southern Illinois.* Cultural Resources Management Report No. 135, American Resources Group, Ltd., Carbondale, Illinois.

McDavid, Carol, and David W. Babson (editors). 1997. In the Realm of Politics: Prospects for Public Participation in African-American and Plantation Archaeology. *Historical Archaeology* 31(3).

McMurry, Sally. 1988. *Families and Farmhouses in Nineteenth Century America: Vernacular Design and Social Change.* Oxford University Press, New York.

———. 1995. *Transforming Rural Life: Dairying Families and Agricultural Change, 1820–1885*. Johns Hopkins University Press, Baltimore, Maryland.

Moir, Randall W., and David H. Jurney (editors). 1987. *Pioneer Settlers, Tenant Farmers, and Communities: Objectives, Historical Background, and Excavations*. Richland Creek Technical Series, Volume IV. Archaeology Research Program, Institute for the Study of Earth and Man, Southern Methodist University, Dallas, Texas.

Morgan, John. 1990. *The Log House in East Tennessee*. University of Tennessee Press, Knoxville.

Mullins, Paul R. 1999. *Race and Affluence: An Archaeology of African America and Consumer Culture*. Kluwer Academic/Plenum Publishers, New York.

Nassaney, Michael. 1998. *Historical Archaeology in Battle Creek: The 1996 Field Season at the Warren B. Shepard Site (20CA104)*. Archaeological Report No. 20. Department of Anthropology, Western Michigan University, Kalamazoo.

Nassaney, Michael, and C. Nickolai. 1999. Selective Memories and the Material World: The Changing Significance of the Warren B. Shepard Site, Battle Creek, Michigan. *Material History Review* 50: 76–85.

Nassaney, Michael S., Deborah L. Rotman, Daniel O. Sayers, and Carol A. Nickolai. 2001. The Southwest Michigan Historical Landscape Project: Exploring Class, Gender, and Ethnicity from the Ground Up. *International Journal of Historical Archaeology* 5(3): 219–261.

Nöel Hume, Ivor. 1982. *Martin's Hundred: The Discovery of a Lost Colonial Virginia Settlement*. Dell Publishing, New York.

Norris, F. Terry. 1991. Ste. Genevieve, a French Colonial Village in the Illinois Country. In *French Colonial Archaeology: The Illinois Country and the Western Great Lakes*, edited by John A. Walthall, pp. 133–148. University of Illinois Press, Urbana.

Orser, Charles E., Jr. 1988a. *The Material Basis of the Postbellum Plantation: Historical Archaeology in the South Carolina Piedmont*. University of Georgia Press, Athens.

———. 1988b. The Archaeological Analysis of Plantation Society: Replacing Status and Caste with Economics and Power. *American Antiquity* 53(4): 735–751.

———. 1996. *A Historical Archaeology of the Modern World*. Springer, New York.

———. 1998. The Archaeology of the African Diaspora. *Annual Review of Anthropology* 27: 63–82.

———(editor). 1990. Historical Archaeology on Southern Plantations and Farms. *Historical Archaeology* 24(4).

Paynter, Robert. 1982. *Models of Spatial Inequality: Settlement Patterns in Historical Archaeology*. Academic Press, New York.

Petraglia, Michael D., Dennis A. Knepper, Christopher Martin, and Mara E. Rosenthal. 1992a. Phase I Survey and Phase II Testing Along the CNG Natural Gas Pipeline (TL-400 Extension 1), Beaver, Butler, and Armstrong Counties, Pennsylvania. Ms. on file, Bureau for Historic Preservation, Harrisburg, Pennsylvania.

Petraglia, Michael D., Dennis A. Knepper, Christopher Martin, Holly Heston, Madeleine Pappas, and Francis Alexander. 1992b. Phase II Testing and Additional Phase I Survey Along the CNG Natural Gas Pipeline (TL-400 Extension 1), Beaver, Butler, and

Armstrong Counties, Pennsylvania. Ms. on file, Bureau for Historic Preservation, Harrisburg, Pennsylvania.

Phillippe, Joseph S. 1990. *The Drake Site: Subsistence and Status at a Rural Illinois Farmstead*. Midwestern Archaeological Research Center, Illinois State University, Normal.

Preston, P.W. 1982. *Theories of Development*. Routledge, Kegan, and Paul, Boston, Massachusetts.

Pursell, Carroll. 2001. *American Technology (Blackwell Readers in American Social and Cultural History)*. Blackwell Publishers, Malden, Massachusetts.

Rafferty, Seán M. 1996. *Data Recovery Plan, The Porter Site, SUBi-1533, NYSM #10074, PIN 9102.11.102, Route 235 over Wylie Brook, Town of Coventry, Chenango County, New York*. Report prepared for the New York State Museum, State Education Department by Public Archaeology Facility, State University of New York at Binghamton.

———. 2000. A Farmhouse View: The Porter Site. In *Nineteenth- and Early Twentieth-Century Domestic Site Archaeology in New York State*, edited by John P. Hart and Charles L. Fisher, pp. 125–147. New York State Museum Bulletin 495. University of the State of New York and the State Education Department, Albany.

Reitz, E. J., T. Gibbs, and T. A. Rathbun. 1985. Archaeological Evidence for Subsistence on Coastal Plantations. In *The Archaeology of Slavery and Plantation Life*, edited by T. A. Singleton, pp. 163–191. Academic Press, New York.

Rostow, W. W. 1960. *The Stages of Economic Growth: A Non-Communist Manifesto*. Cambridge University Press, New York.

Rotman, Deborah L. 1995. Class and Gender in Southwestern Michigan: Interpreting Historical Landscapes. Unpublished Master's thesis, Department of Anthropology, Western Michigan University, Kalamazoo.

Rotman, Deborah L., and Michael Nassaney. 1997. Class, Gender, and the Built Environment: Deriving Social Relations from Cultural Landscapes in Southwest Michigan. *Historical Archaeology* 31(2): 42–62.

Sanderson, Stephen K. 1995. *Social Transformations: A General Theory of Historical Development*. Blackwell, Cambridge, Massachusetts.

Sayers, Daniel O. 1999. Of Agrarian Landscapes and Capitalist Transitions: Historical Archaeology and the Political Economy of a Nineteenth-Century Farmstead. Master's thesis, Department of Anthropology, Western Michigan University, Kalamazoo.

———. 2003. Glimpses Into the Dialectics of Antebellum Landscape Nucleation in Agrarian Michigan. *Journal of Archaeological Method and Theory* 10(4): 369–432.

Sayers, Daniel O., and Michael Nassaney. 1999. Antebellum Landscapes and Agrarian Political Economies: Modeling Progressive Farmsteads in Southwest Michigan. *The Michigan Archaeologist* 45(3): 74–117.

Schlereth, Thomas J. 1992. *Victorian American: Transformation in Everyday Life, 1876–1915*. Harper Perennial, New York.

Singleton, Theresa A. 1988. An Archaeological Framework for Slavery and Emancipation, 1740–1880. In *The Recovery of Meaning: Historical Archaeology in the Eastern United States*, edited by Mark P. Leone and Parker B. Potter, Jr., pp. 345–370. Smithsonian Institution Press, Washington, D.C.

————. 1995. The Archaeology of Slavery in North America. *Annual Review of Anthropology* 24: 119–140.

————. 2001. *"I, Too, Am America": Archaeological Studies of African-American Life*. University of Virginia Press, Charlottesville.

Singleton, Theresa A., and Mark D. Bograd. 1995. *The Archaeology of the African Diaspora in the Americas*. Guides to the Archaeological Literature of the Immigrant Experiences in America 2. The Society for Historical Archaeology, California, Pennsylvania.

Smith, Samuel D. 1996. *A Bibliographic History of Historical Archaeology in Tennessee*. Miscellaneous Publication No. 4, Tennessee Department of Environment and Conservation, Division of Archaeology, Nashville.

Smith, Steven D. 1993. *Made it in the Timber: A Historic Overview of the Fort Leonard Wood Region, 1800–1940*. Report Prepared by Midwestern Archaeological Research Center, Illinois State University, Normal. Prepared for the U.S. Army Corps of Engineers, Kansas City District.

So, Alvin Y. 1990. *Social Change and Development: Modernization, Dependency, and World-System Theories*. Sage Library of Social Research. Sage Publications, Thousand Oaks, California.

South, Stanley. 1988. Santa Elena: Threshold of Conquest. In *The Recovery of Meaning: Historical Archaeology in the Eastern United States*, edited by Mark P. Leone and Parker B. Potter, Jr., pp. 27–140. Smithsonian Institution Press, Washington, D.C.

Stewart-Abernathy, Leslie C. 1986. *The Moser Farmstead, Independent But Not Isolated: The Archaeology of a Late Nineteenth Century Ozark Farmstead*. Arkansas Archeological Survey Research Series No. 26. University of Arkansas, Fayetteville.

Stine, Linda France. 1989. Raised Up in Hard Times, Circa 1900–1940. Unpublished Ph.D. dissertation, Department of Anthropology, University of North Carolina, Chapel Hill.

————. 1990. Social Inequality and Turn-of-the-Century Farmsteads: Issues of Class, Status, Ethnicity, and Race. *Historical Archaeology* 24(4): 37–49.

Stine, Linda France, Melanie A. Cabak, and Mark D. Groover. 1996. Blue Beads as African-American Cultural Symbols. *Historical Archaeology* 30(3): 49–75.

————. 2000. Blue Beads as African-American Cultural Symbols. In *Approaches to Material Culture Research for Historical Archaeologists*, 2nd edition, compiled by David R. Brauner, pp. 221–247. Society for Historical Archaeology, Uniontown, Pennsylvania.

Stine, Linda France, Martha Zierden, Lesley Drucker, and Christopher Judge. 1997. *Carolina's Historical Landscapes: Archaeological Perspectives*. University of Tennessee Press, Knoxville.

Symons, Leslie. 1979. *Agricultural Geography*. Westview Press, Boulder, Colorado.

Tarrant, John R. 1974. *Agricultural Geography*. John Wiley and Sons, New York.

Terrill, Tom E., and Jerrold Hirsch (editors). 1978. *Such as Us: Southern Voices of the Thirties*. W. W. Norton, New York.

Trimble, Michael K., Teresita Majewski, Michael J. O'Brien, and Anna L. Price. 1991. Frontier Colonization of the Saline Creek Valley. In *French Colonial Archaeology: The*

Illinois Country and the Western Great Lakes, edited by John A. Walthall, pp. 165–188. University of Illinois Press, Urbana.

United States Bureau of the Census (USBC). 1853. *Seventh Census of the United States: 1850*. Robert Armstrong, Washington, D.C.

United States Department of Agriculture (USDA). 1997. *Census of Agriculture*. Government Printing Office, Washington, D.C.

———. 2002. *Census of Agriculture*. Government Printing Office, Washington, D.C.

United States Department of Commerce (USDC). 1913. *Thirteenth Census of the United States, Taken in the Year 1910*, Volume VII, *Agriculture, 1909 and 1910*. Government Printing Office, Washington, D.C.

———. 1922. *Fourteenth Census of the United States: 1920, Agriculture*. Government Printing Office, Washington, D.C.

———. 1932. *Fifteenth Census of the United States: 1930, Agriculture*. Government Printing Office, Washington, D.C.

———. 1942. *Sixteenth Census of the United States: 1940, Agriculture*. Government Printing Office, Washington, D.C.

———. 1952. *United States Census of Agriculture: 1950*. Government Printing Office, Washington, D.C.

———. 1959. *United States Census of Agriculture*. Government Printing Office, Washington, D.C.

———. 1964. *United States Census of Agriculture*. Government Printing Office, Washington, D.C.

———. 1982. *United States Census of Agriculture*. Government Printing Office, Washington , D.C.

United States Department of Interior (USDI). 1864. *Agriculture of the United States in 1860: Compiled from the Original Returns of the Eighth Census*. Government Printing Office, Washington, D.C.

———. 1872. *Ninth Census*, Volume III: *The Statistics of the Wealth and Industry of the United States: 1870*. Government Printing Office, Washington, D.C.

———. 1883. *Report of the Production of Agriculture as Returned at the Tenth Census: 1880*. Government Printing Office, Washington, D.C.

———. 1895. *Report on the Statistics of Agriculture in the United States at the Eleventh Census: 1890*. Government Printing Office, Washington, D.C.

———. 1902. *Census Reports, Volume V, Twelfth Census of the United States, Taken in the Year 1900, Agriculture*, Part I: *Farms, Live Stock, and Animal Products*. Government Printing Office, Washington, D.C.

Veblen, Thorstein. 1973. *The Theory of the Leisure Class*. Houghton Mifflin, Boston.

Vlach, John Michael. 1976. The Shotgun House: An African Legacy. *Pioneer America* 8: 47–80.

Walker, H. J., and W. G. Haag (editors). 1974. *Man and Cultural Heritage: Papers in Honor of Fred B. Kniffen*. Geoscience and Man 5. Louisiana State University School of Geoscience, Baton Rouge.

Wallerstein, Immanuel. 1974. *The Modern World-System I*. Academic Press, New York.

———. 1980. *The Modern World-System II*. Academic Press, New York.

———. 1984. Long Waves as Capitalist Process. *Review* 7:559–575.

———. 1989. *The Modern World-System III*. Academic Press, New York.

Walthall, John A. 1991. French Colonial Fort Massac: Architecture and Ceramic Patterning. In *French Colonial Archaeology: The Illinois Country and the Western Great Lakes*, edited by John A. Walthall, pp. 42–64. University of Illinois Press, Urbana.

Walthall, John A., and Thomas E. Emerson. 1991. French Colonial Archaeology. In *French Colonial Archaeology: The Illinois Country and the Western Great Lakes*, edited by John A. Walthall, pp. 1–13. University of Illinois Press, Urbana.

Wilkie, Laurie. 2003. *The Archaeology of Mothering: An African-American Midwife's Tale*. Routledge Press, New York.

Williams, Susan. 2006. *Food in the United States, 1820s–1890*. Greenwood Press, Westport, Connecticut.

Wilson, Eugene M. 1975. *American Folk Houses*. Alabama Historical Commission, Montgomery.

Wilson, John S. 1990. We've Got Thousands of These! What Makes an Historic Farmstead Significant? *Historical Archaeology* 24(2): 23–33.

Wolf, Eric R. 1982. *Europe and the People Without History*. University of California Press, Berkeley.

Woodman, Harold D. 1997. Class, Race, Politics, and the Modernization of the Postbellum South. *Journal of Southern History* 63(1): 3–22.

Wright, Gavin. 1986. *Old South, New South: Revolutions in the Southern Economy Since the Civil War*. Basic Books, New York.

Yamin, Rebecca, and Karen Bescherer Metheny. 1996. *Landscape Archaeology: Reading and Interpreting the American Historical Landscape*. University of Tennessee Press, Knoxville.

Index

Page numbers in italics refer to illustrations.

Mark D. Groover, a historical archaeologist, is associate professor of anthropology at Ball State University. He has written a book, journal articles, and numerous excavation reports about the historical archaeology of farmsteads and plantations.